The NEATS

A Child & Family Assessment

*Neurobiology, Executive function,
Attachment, Trauma, & Self-regulation*

Copyright © 2011 by Jane Gilgun

jgilgun@gmail.com

The NEATS: A Child & Family Assessment
by Jane Gilgun
Third Edition
193 pages

ISBN 10: 1-4662-8009-3
ISBN 13: 978-1-4662-8009-0

1. social work 2. assessment 3. case plans 4. neurobiology 5. executive function 6. attachment 7. trauma 8. self-regulation 9. parenting 10. families 11. children's mental health

Includes Further Readings and Internet Resources

The NEATS

A Child & Family Assessment

Neurobiology, Executive function, Attachment, Trauma, & Self-regulation

Jane F. Gilgun, Ph.D., LICSW

Also by Jane Gilgun

Children's Books
Busjacked!
Daddy Loves Me
Emma and her Forever Person
Five Little Cygnets Cross the Bundoran Road
The King's Toast
The Little Pig Who Didn't go to Market
Salamander: A Story of Two Boys
Turtle Night at Playa Grande
Will the Soccer Star

Books
Child Sexual Abuse: From Harsh Realities to Hope
Children with Serious Conduct Issues
I Want to Show You: Poems
Landscapes of Northwest Ireland & Other Places Called Home: Photographs
On Being a Shit: Unkind Deeds & Cover-Ups in Everyday Life

Short Pieces
Attachment & Child Development
Detecting the Potential for Violence
Executive Function & Self-Regulation in Children
Family Incest Treatment & Professional Treatment for Abusers
Neurobiology, Trauma, & Child Development
Preventing the Development of Sexually Abusive Behaviors
Remove Offending Priests Immediately: What was the Bishop Thinking?
Secondary Trauma as an Occupational Hazard for Social Service Professionals
Talking to Children Who Have Been Sexually Abused
The Sex Education of Children
Two Boys, Similar Backgrounds: One Goes to Prison & One Does Not: Why?
Victim-Blaming in Child Sexual Abuse Cases
What Sexual Abuse Means to Child Survivors
What Sexual Abuse Means to Abusers
What Child Sexual Abuse Means to Girl & Women Perpetrators

Periodicals
Current Issues in Qualitative Research
Roots of Violence, Seeds of Change
The OBS Express

Preface

The NEATS is a child and family assessment that directs practitioner attention to five areas of human development and functioning that research has established as fundamental. These areas are neurobiology, executive function, attachment, trauma, and self-regulation. The title *NEATS* draws from the first letter of each of the five areas. The assessment is competency-based and ecological. It guides practitioners to identify resources, strengths, competencies, and resilience within the ecologies in which children and families live their lives.

These ecologies include families, extended families, neighborhoods, peer groups, social networks, schools, and the influences of social services, community resources, and social policies. Considerations of opportunities and access issues related to race, gender, ethnicity, socioeconomic status, ability, and religion are also part of the assessment.

I developed the NEATS through research, practice, teaching and consultation. The NEATS prepares professionals to do sound assessments on which to base case plans. These professionals include social workers, case managers, psychologists, counselors, nurses, psychiatrists and other medical doctors. Parents who participate in professional services with their children may also find this book helpful.

Children thrive when they feel safe and engage in reciprocal relationships of love and care. Safety is ensured when adults provide routines and structure, are clear in their expectations, recognize and praise appropriate behaviors, explain reasons for rules, and provide guidance for alternative behaviors when children behave inappropriately. Adults have power over children. Children are safe when adults recognize their power and use it to promote children's well-being. Some children also seem to have incredible skill in how to push parents' buttons. The NEATS assessment guides practitioners to develop case plans that provide opportunities for children and their parents to reach their potential, recognizing that neurological conditions may affect human potential.

The first six chapters of the book describe the NEATS. Chapters 7 and 8 show applications of the NEATS to case studies, chapters 9 through 13 provide a NEATS analysis of common childhood issues, while chapter 14 provides guidelines for comprehensive case planning. References, further readings, and internet resources are present after some of the chapters and at the end of the book.

Jane F. Gilgun
Minneapolis, Minnesota, USA
August 30, 2011

Acknowledgements

Many thanks to Danette Jones and Sue Keskinen for their long-term collaborations. Thanks, too, to the administrators and staff, both past and present, of the All Children Excel Program (ACE), which is an agency of the Ramsey County, Minnesota, USA, Human Services and Public Health Departments. They along with Danette helped me think about and apply the concepts of the NEATS. These professionals are Ed Frickson, Hope Melton, Jody McElroy, Roy Adams, Mary McRoy, Leslie Norsted, Jack Jones, Dave Wilmes, Nancy LeTourneau, Antuana Belton, Carlos Stewart, Rebecca Muotka, Dylan DePrimo, Troy Withers, Gala Ingram, Carlton Linton, and Betsy Brewer.

My four-year experience with the advisory board of the Hennepin County Adoption Project, Hennepin County, Minnesota, USA, and with Ginny Blade of the North American Council on Adoptable Children, St. Paul, Minnesota, contributed to the writing of this book.

My ongoing research projects on how persons over come adversities have provided rich understandings for this book. I want to thank the many people who have worked with me on these projects.

Contents

1

Description of the NEATS

The NEATS is a child and family assessment that focuses on five areas that research has established as fundamental to human functioning and development. These areas are neurobiology, executive function, attachment, trauma, and self regulation. The title *NEATS* draws from the first letter of each of the five areas.

The five elements of the NEATS are inter-related. For example, neurobiology provides a foundation for the development of attachment relationships and executive functions. Secure attachment relationships, in turn, are the basis of optimal brain development and help to build executive skills based on the foundation that neurobiology provides. Executive functions include judgment, planning, and capacities for the management of emotions and the effects of trauma. Furthermore, negative experiences such as trauma, loss, and neglect, can affect brain development as well as capacities for attachment, self-regulation, and executive function. What affects one dimension of the NEATS affects them all.

The purpose of a NEATS assessment is to develop comprehensive case plans. To do so, practitioners identify risks and adversities as well as resources, competencies, strengths, and resilience processes that affect families and children. This involves assessing not only the children, but their parents, siblings, extended family, school and community settings, neighborhood, peer group, the effects of social policies and other historical forces, and any number of other influences on child functioning. The point is to find areas of strengths and relationships that contribute to positive child and family experiences and to identify areas that undermine child and family functioning.

An ecomap illustrates these multiple influences. Figure 1 shows an ecomap.

Figure 1: An Ecomap for Children & Families

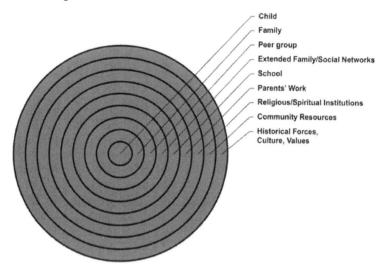

- Child
- Family
- Peer group
- Extended Family/Social Networks
- School
- Parents' Work
- Religious/Spiritual Institutions
- Community Resources
- Historical Forces, Culture, Values

Family history is important in a NEATS assessment. Therefore, practitioners can create a second ecomap that represent family experiences during significant times in the past, such as when things were going well, or when there was an event or series of events that undermined family functioning.

Genograms can be helpful in a NEATS assessment. Genograms, or family trees, map family characteristics over two or more generations. They are an efficient way to organize information. Figure 2 shows a genogram. Many issues that affect children are issues that are present in other family members, including parents, siblings, grandparents, parents' siblings, and cousins. Sometimes this transmission appears to be genetic, other times related to family experiences, and sometimes a combination.

Figure 2: A Three Generational Genogram

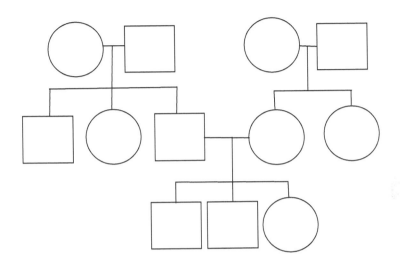

For example, when children are diagnosed with ADHD or an anxiety disorder, there may be other family members within the child's generation or in previous generations who also had ADHD or anxiety disorders. These conditions may be results of genetics. Criminal behaviors that appear across generations may result from patterns of family interaction and modeling. Such behaviors probably are not inheritable but arise from environmental influences. Still other conditions, such as alcoholism may have both genetic and environmental origins.

Purposes of a NEATS Assessment

The NEATS is designed for practice with children and families, such as child protection, mental health, child and family services, youth corrections, and parent education. The NEATS alerts practitioners to important areas of child and family functioning and provides fundamental information about them. The NEATS reminds practitioners of what is important and helps them to avoid falling back on what they have always assessed. Parents may find the NEATS helps them to understand their children and themselves.

The NEATS is not a diagnostic tool. Diagnoses, such as those related to neurology and mental health, require specialized expertise that may be both medical and technological. Rather than diagnosing, the NEATS guides practitioners to seek basic information about the five areas of functioning that practitioners can use to guide their next steps in case planning. These steps include planning for how to acquire additional information, for seeking further collaborations, and for making referrals. The NEATS organizes a great deal of information and provides a focus for case plans. A comprehensive service plan results because the NEATS leads practitioners to assess the multiple influences on families, as discussed earlier.

Case plans that result from a NEATS assessment are much more likely to be effective if service providers first ensure that clients' basic human needs are met. These basic human needs include adequate food, safety, clothing, shelter, medical care, and stability. Sometimes services must be provided even when human needs go unmet. Case plans, no matter how grounded in comprehensive assessments, may not be achievable under these conditions.

2

Neurobiology

Neurobiology is a branch of biology concerned with the anatomy and physiology of the nervous system, especially the brain, under various conditions of health, stress, and pathology. Neurobiological systems are the foundation for how we think, feel, and behave, while simultaneously, how we think, feel, and behave shapes the workings of our brains. Who we are as human beings is inseparable from how our brains work.

Neurobiology provides the basis for the formation of attachment relationships with care providers and also shapes children's capacities for planning and judgment and for managing emotions and trauma. These capacities are foundational to growth and development.

Neurobiology has become so important that some researchers believe that the integration of neuroscience with social work practice will determine which social service organizations will be effective and which will be ineffective. Whether agencies will be winners and losers in the eyes of funders as well as with the general public may depend on this integration.

Practitioners who do assessments using the NEATS must have basic knowledge of the neurological foundations of childhood conditions, an understanding of their origins, and familiarity with effective interventions and referral sources for these conditions.

Unfortunately, some of these services are hard to come by for people in rural areas. Even in urban and suburban areas, adequate services may be in short supply because of a national shortage of child psychiatrists and pediatric neurologists. Social policy and programs have not yet caught on to the need for readily available services for children with neurological difficulties.

Basic Notions

Children are born with billions more brain cells, called neurons, than then they will ever use. Which neurons are kept, which are shed, and which develop into brain circuits that connect various parts of the brain depend upon experience and genetics. For example, children whose parents provide them with sensitive, responsive care will develop brain circuits that encode expectations that others will treat them well and will develop positive self-concepts. They also will develop capacities for sensitivity and caring for others and will encode these capacities in brain circuits. Such children are likely to develop good social skills, cooperate with adult directives, and persist when tasks challenge them.

This is the principle of from external to internal to external, where environmental influences such as sensitive parenting are internalized and that children in turn externalize in their own actions. This also illustrates mirroring where children imitate and internalize how they were treated. How they treat others and how they conduct themselves in the world depends on how significant others treated them.

Physical touch, love, sensitive and reciprocal interactions with care providers and others and sensory stimulation promote optimal brain development, as well as social, emotional, and physical development. Infants and young children who are talked to and provided with other age-appropriate stimulation will encode these experiences that in turn will help them develop verbal skills and other capacities that enhance their brain's healthy development and their social and emotional development. A characteristic of brains, then, is plasticity, meaning that sensitive, responsive care and other environmental events shape brain development.

Some children are born with neurological conditions that place limits on how their brains develop. With sensitive, responsive care, these children will develop optimally, but some conditions permanently cause difficulties in functioning. Ceiling effects is the term used when there are upper limits to the brain's capacity for development.

In general, brain functioning stems from both genetics and environmental influences. Genetics provides infants with innate capacities that are shaped by experience. Genetics can predispose children to neurological difficulties, but inadequate prenatal care, including poor nutrition and the ingestion of drugs and alcohol during pregnancy, also can influence brain development. Birth accidents, such as ingestion of amniotic fluids that late in pregnancy also contain fetal waste products, can affect neurological functioning. Trauma and stress can harm brain development and even kill some brain cells.

Children whose neurological development has been affected by trauma or physical injury can, with optimal care, develop new brain circuits. Furthermore, other parts of the brain can "take over" the functions of damaged areas. These findings lend further support to the idea that the brain is plastic; that is, capable of change and adaptation, although there are limits to brain development, called ceiling effects, as already discussed.

Thus, children can recover to varying degrees from physical and psychological trauma, but this takes a major commitment on the part of parents and other attachment figures to do so. Attachment figures must be willing to do whatever it takes on behalf of their children to help the children process past and present events in their lives. They must have capacities to change their own behaviors and expectations to help the children.

Unfortunately, some parents cannot do this. They may refuse to believe their behaviors affect their children, and they may refuse services that could support them in efforts to promote their children's optimal development. In addition, some parents might not even know these services exist. Finally, sometimes the services they receive are inadequate. Savvy service providers have a major responsibility to identify appropriate services. Policy makers and the general public have the responsibility to ensure that adequate and appropriate services exist.

Common Neurological Conditions

Conditions that result from compromised brain functioning include autism spectrum disorders, fetal alcohol effects, attention deficit hyperactivity disorders, depression, anxiety disorders, bipolar disorders, Tourette's, and some forms of oppositional behaviors, among others.

Often a combination of medications, psychoeducation, the meeting of basic human needs, optimization of parents' mental health, parent support groups, and psychotherapy can enhance the functioning of children with neurological conditions. Pediatric neurologists, child psychiatrists, and child neuropsychologists would be important members of teams that work with children and families where children have neurological issues.

Important recent research shows that with early intervention, children born with autism can develop new neural capacities that alter the course of the syndrome. Early intervention with children who have experienced the trauma of abuse and neglect can also gain or regain optimal neurological functioning. These findings show the brain's capacity to change and that experience shape brain development.

Children with neurological issues typically receive special education and have individual educational plans at school. School personnel want parents to be involved with these educational plans and can contribute a great deal to them. Parents, sometimes confused and frustrated with their relationships to school personnel, may appreciate the advocacy efforts that professionals can make on behalf of their children. Likewise, teachers frequently appreciate the support and information that knowledgeable social service professionals offer.

Parents Require Specialized Help

Children who have issues related to neurobiology may be challenging. Parents require specialized help to meet these changes. Experts in child neurology and psychology can provide guidance and care. These professionals include psychologists, psychiatrists, pediatric neurologists, and mental health specialists with training and experience in the area of child neurology

Parent support groups can be a source of empathy, emotional support, and information that can give parents' strategies for dealing with their children and validation of their worth and efforts as parents. Day care and respite care can be of great help. In addition, personal care attendants who stay with children while in school can provide structure and support when children cannot manage their behaviors unassisted.

In some situations, even with the best of care, children's capacities may be limited because of their neurological make-up. As discussed earlier, the term "ceiling effect" stands for situations where children cannot progress beyond a certain point. For instance, the effects of alcohol on fetal brain development produces such ceiling effects even with the best of care.

Far-Reaching Effects of Neurological Conditions

Family stress, marital discord, and job issues related to child care are common in families with a child or children with difficult neurologically-based challenges. Other children in the family can be affected. Without realizing it, parents may not attend consistently to the needs of siblings because of their focus on a child with neurological issues. Parents may be too worn out themselves to realize that the other children feel left out.

The relationship between other children and a child with neurological issues must be monitored carefully, too. Sibling relationships contribute to children's capacities to form relationships with others as well as their sense of who they are, what they deserve, how others should treat them, and how they relate to others. The centrality of relationships is discussed in more detail in the section on attachment.

These are relatively new learnings that are an important part of competent service provision. In the past, children's difficulties were assumed to be the result of inadequate parenting, particularly mothering. Now, neuroscience has taught us that some behaviors are related to brain structure and function. While some behaviors are amenable to change under optimal conditions, others are not, no matter how competent the care.

In short, children's neurobiological makeup is the foundation for the development of capacities for attachment, executive function, and self-regulation. Conversely, trauma, neglectful attachment figures, and inadequate care can negatively affect children's neurological functioning. Parents of children with neurological challenges require supportive services. Professional services can contribute significantly to children's optimal development.

Practice Note

Neurological conditions such as autism spectrum disorders, bi-polar disorders, schizophrenia, and attention deficit hyperactivity disorder (ADHD) typically are transmitted genetically, although there are exceptions. When children have neurological issues, best practice leads to assessing parents, grandparents, and other family members for neurological issues. As part of the assessment, therefore, family trees or genograms can help identity the transmission of neurological conditions. Medical histories contained in genograms can help medical doctors and other service providers make accurate diagnoses and thus to develop helpful treatment plans.

For example, Jack is a six-year old boy whose explosive behaviors are so extreme that they require containment several times a day. A genogram showed that Jack's father was diagnosed with schizophrenia and his mother with bipolar disorder. Jack could have inherited a predisposition for a neurological condition.

A thorough NEATS assessment would require a review of the other four elements of the NEATS to get an idea of the contributions of parenting styles and family life to Jack's behavioral issues. If the parents manage their conditions well, there is reason to be optimistic about Jack's long-term outcome. However, if parents' conditions are untreated and unmanaged, chances are parents will be unable to provide stability and consistency of love and care that children require to develop well.

Sometimes children's behaviors appear to be neurologically based, but could be the results of unattended trauma and other adversities, such as chaotic parenting. Using ADHD as an example again, symptoms of this condition can also be symptoms of trauma. Evaluations by neuropsychologists, pediatric neurologists, or child psychiatrist could help make these distinctions. The symptoms must be treated but any final diagnosis must be withheld until the evidence supports it.

Trauma and family chaos may affect children's brain development, but a structured treatment plan remains the approach of choice no matter the origins. A key part of a treatment plan is for parents to manage their own issues, whatever they may be.

A great deal of information is required for an accurate assessment and the formulation of an effective treatment plan when children appear to have neurological issues. Part of the treatment plan is a referral to professionals trained in neurobiology. They will do further evaluations in order to make conclusions about possible diagnoses.

Neurobiology affects many areas of child and family functioning. To do sound assessments, practitioners must have a good understanding of what each of the components of the NEATS means.

3

Executive Function

Executive function (EF) is a term that covers a broad range of capacities related to judgment, problem-solving, organization of self, anticipation of consequences, working memory, and following rules and directions. Regulation of emotions, thoughts, and behaviors is part of executive function as well, but in the NEATS assessment, self-regulation is a separate category because of its significance in social work and other applied settings.

The neurological basis of executive function is located primarily in the prefrontal cortex, which is in the front of the brain and is the seat of reasoning. The term "executive" fits these sets of capacities because an executive is someone who is in charge. The prefrontal cortex, however, is connected to many other areas of the brain, such as emotion and motor centers.

Like brain functioning in general, executive functions or skills arise from a combination of genetics and experience. Adequate nutrition and good prenatal care as well as genetics lead to good executive functions at birth. Subsequent experience contributes further to executive function development. With sensitive, responsive care, children build upon existing skills to continue their optimal development.

Stress, trauma, abuse, and neglect may undermine the development of executive skills in children with a good genetic makeup. These children can recover or develop new executive skills if their circumstances change for the better, where parenting is sensitive and responsive, except if the damage to neural circuits cannot be reversed.

Conversely, many children are born with brain functions that predispose them to executive function issues, but their quality of care is so high that they develop new neural circuits that appear to compensate for what might have been executive function deficits. How much neural growth is possible is related to genetic makeup and whether or not any brain damage has ceiling effects. For example, there appear to be ceiling effects for some of the executive functions of children with fetal alcohol effects.

Parents of children with executive function challenges may require emotional support and psychoeducation and the children's development of executive skills could take longer than with other children. Once again, however, there are limits to the brain's plasticity and some individuals may have life-long issues with executive functions.

Conditions Associated with Executive Function

Executive function issues include difficulties with attention, following directions and rules, organizing the self, self-soothing when stressed, and self-regulation, and impulse control. Impulse control and following involves capacities for holding information in working memory and in considering alternatives and consequences, as well as resistance to distractions.

Childhood issues connected to problems in executive function issues are those listed under "neurobiology," including fetal alcohol spectrum disorders, autism spectrum disorders, conduct disorders, oppositional disorders, and attention deficit/hyperactivity disorders (ADHD). In general, children may have good executive skills in some situations and not in others.

Children with executive function issues require structure in their daily lives, clear and simple directions in how to accomplish tasks, clear expectations, and heaps of praise when they show the smallest executive skill. They benefit when others show them how to do things and when the adults around them also have good executive skills.

As with other challenging child behaviors, parents of children with executive function issues benefit from psychoeducation, parent support groups, and professionals who themselves have good executive skills. Parents' executive functions are compromised if they have chemical dependency issues and untreated mental illness.

Practice Note

Once practitioners have reason to believe that children have executive function issues, it is advisable to assess parents' executive functions. Children learn good executive skills from their everyday experiences of care that parents and others provide. The case of six year-old Jack who has a diagnosis of ADHD will illustrate this point. Almost by definition, executive function issues are part of ADHD. To develop an effective treatment plan for Jack, practitioners would assess parents for executive function skills as well and then recommend a course of action for them if they have executive function issues. Typical referrals are parenting classes, parent support groups, and psychotherapy, which can be a combination of individual, family, and couple treatment.

Another important application of the concept of executive function is to assess who is in charge of the family; in other words, who has the executive functions for the family. In traditional families, where fathers and husbands are in charge of household finances and child discipline, women may struggle with executive function issues if their husbands die or leave the family. An older child may assume executive roles, but not have the skills to fulfill them.

For example, Pang, a Hmong refugee, a widow, and the mother of six children ages sixteen to six, depended upon her sixteen year-old daughter Moa to use the cash card that county social services agency provided every month. Pang did not know how to use the card and asked Moa to do it. Moa spent the money on clothes and entertainment for herself and her friends, leaving the family in serious financial difficulties, and showing her poor executive functions in this situation. An effective treatment plan would assist Pang in taking on executive functions.

4

Attachment

A ttachment is defined as behaviors that maintain contact with care providers who serve as a secure base from which to explore and to which to return under times of stress, as well as to serve as a source of nurturance, love and affirmation. Attachment is also a process, whose outward characteristics change as children grow and develop, but at its core attachment is a source of nurturance, problem-solving, affirmation, and even courage to try new things or to persist when times are tough.

Attachment relationships contribute to brain development, executive function, and self-regulation, including the regulation of stress and trauma. Without repair, breakdown in attachment relationships in infancy and childhood may have life-long effects.

Qualities associated with attachment also include reciprocity, attunement, and contingent responsiveness. Attachment is a complex set of processes. If professionals are to do effective assessments and case plans, they must have a good grasp of its complexities.

An example of attachment as process in infancy is when a child has a wet diaper and is uncomfortable. The child signals discomfort to the care provider through crying and other signs of distress. The care provider responds by figuring out what is causing the distress, removes the soiled diaper, washes the baby, and provides the baby with a fresh diaper.

These simple acts soothe the child's stress and affirm for the child that his or her bids for care will be attended to. Care providers feel

15

satisfaction not only in the child's positive responses to being attended to, but also because the child stops crying. Some evolutionary biologists believe that infant crying is aversive. When parental care stops the crying and the infant is happy, these actions are satisfying to care providers. This is a mutually satisfying interaction that ensures that parents will care for children. In terms of evolutionary biology, attachment behaviors are necessary for survival.

Caregiver Attunement and Self-Regulation

As this example suggests, caregiver attunement to what children want and need builds secure attachments. Sometimes children do not want to interact with care providers and turn away. They have had enough interaction for the time being. They may be feeling over-stimulated or tired and want to re-regulate themselves into a more comfortable state.

Sensitive, attuned care providers notice this turning away and re-spect it. They allow children to regulate the duration and intensity of the interactions. In this way, children learn they have power and control to regulate interactions with others. When care providers respect children's wishes, children's stress levels go down. This brings comfort and relief.

Care provider attunement helps children to learn to regulate themselves. This includes regulation of the intensity of their emotions, physiological responses of fatigue and possibly heart rate and pulse, and behaviors. Children who develop capacities for self-regulation will have capacities to be attuned to others and to help others self-regulate.

The development of self-regulation through reciprocal, at-tuned relationships with parents is an example of the external to internal to external principle in child development. Children internalize their experiences, which are encoded in brain circuits. They in turn, exhibit the behaviors that they have experienced. This is the idea behind the principle that children live what they have learned.

Repair

Repair is another idea related to attachment. Care providers can-not always be responsive to children's bids for attention and desires to be left alone. Children cannot always be immediately soothed by the attention, nor can care providers accede to child requests if children are in unsafe situations.

Children who do not get what they want may show their displeasure directly. In secure relationships children trust the stability of their attachments, and they can express both negative and positive emotions without fear. When children protest, attuned parents have opportunities to re-consider their responses. For example, children whose parents are sad and withdrawn may make increasingly vigorous bids for attention. Children have been observed pulling on parents' clothes, patting them on the face, and saying, "Mommy, it's me" when parents are unresponsive.

Responsive parents may realize what they are doing and change their behaviors. This is mutual regulation, this time from child to parent, but it is based on a history of parental responsiveness.

Another example is the actions of toddlers. Their actions must be supervised and corrected. When corrected, children may protest mightily through tantrums and aggression. Such behaviors can lead to temporary breaks in parental attunement and mutual responsiveness. When the tantrum is over, parents and children re-connect and once again become attuned to each other.

Connection, disconnection, repair, and reconnection are characteristic of mutual relationships. Over time, the nature of breaks in relationship change, but the essential quality remains: in secure relationships there are breaks that get repaired. Repair takes place through open expression of points of view and emotions, with adults allowing children to have their say without relinquishing their executive roles of providing safety and guidance.

When repairs are not made, attachment relationships become problematic. Repairs may be rare or even absent when parents and other caregivers are preoccupied with their own issues, dismissive of the significance of children's issues, or so disorganized that they respond in chaotic ways. Families in which partner violence occurs, where there is abuse and neglect, or where childhood traumas are unattended are at high risk for insecure attachments that arise because of lack of repair. Mistrust replaces trust.

Many issues affect parents' capacities for attachment and contingent responsiveness. Highly stressed parents, even those who under normal circumstances cope well, are unlikely to be consistently psychologically available and attuned to their children. Without realizing it, they may not be as attentive to their children as they want to be. Parents with untreated mental illnesses, chemical dependency issues, and unresolved trauma may offer inconsistent and even abusive and neglectful care. Their own issues distract them from attunement with their children.

Variations in Caregiver-Child Attachments

Researchers have identified various styles of attachment that fit individuals as children and as adults. For children, attachments may be secure and insecure. Within the insecure category are avoidant, ambivalent, disorganized, and disordered attachments. For adults, attachments are characterized as secure, and, when parents have traumas in their backgrounds, they are classified as resolved if they manage the trauma well, or as dismissive, preoccupied, and disorganized if they have not.

Adult attachment styles are assumed to have their roots in adults' relationships with their own care providers when they were children. Parent-child attachments typically mirror the kinds of attachments parents have had with their own caregivers.

Secure attachments. Secure attachments in infancy and young childhood are characterized by sensitive, responsive caregiving provided to children who have capacities to respond to such care, with the result that the parent-caregiver relationship is mutually satisfying and promotes optimal child and parent development. The parents of children in secure attachment relationships almost always have parents who secure attachment relationships with their own caregivers.

Children with secure attachments to care providers develop expectation that others will care for them and respond to their needs. They becoming trusting of others and in turn become trustworthy persons themselves.

Insecure attachments. Insecure attachments arise for the most part from inconsistent and detached styles of care giving associated with parental ambivalence, psychological unavailability, or rejection of parental roles. The kinds of insecure attachment relationships that children form roughly mirror their caregivers' own attachment relationships. Sometimes insecure attachments occur even when the caregiving is exemplary, such as when children have undiagnosed, untreated, or untreatable neurological issues or physical and psychological trauma that is left unattended.

Behaviors associated with avoidant attachments include showing little or no emotional responses to parents, little preference for the parents over others, and, over time, difficulty connecting to others and in self-regulation of emotions and behaviors. Children who show these behaviors typically have experienced emotional neglect, which in terms of the previous discussion means that contingent responsiveness and sensitive care were in short supply and psychological unavailability was the norm.

An example of parental statements that suggest avoidant attachment is the following: "They're good kids. They can play all day long without asking me for anything." This is not normal; children and parents interact with each other on and off all day long.

Behaviors associated with ambivalent attachments go from one extreme to the other. Children may show interest in being with parents but also are fearful. Upon being with parents after separation, children may at first be pleased to see them but then struggle to get away.

Disorganized behaviors are similar to ambivalence, but are more extreme and may include approach-avoidance behaviors and rapid changes of mood such as happiness, fear, and anger.

Reactive attachment disorders (RAD) are an extreme form of insecure attachments where the children avoid interaction with others or are indiscriminant in approaching others. RAD arises from pathogenic care, which is serious, chronic deprivation of comfort, interaction, consistency, and sensitivity. Many of the signs of RAD are also signs of trauma. In fact, chronic, multiple traumas are characteristic of RAD.

Insecure attachments are associated with mistrust and can set children up for problematic relationships with others, social isolation, and/or aggressive and other inappropriate behaviors. In some ways, their attachment relationships help "program" their brains so that they behave as if every human being and situation are as untrustworthy as their care providers.

Children with insecure attachments may have had some experience with secure attachments. They thus have some capacities related to trust encoded in their brains. This means that under safe and secure conditions, they may show capacities for attunement and self-regulation. These capacities, however, may be built on fragile ground. Children with these issues require sensitive care that allows them to process their trauma and learn to mange its effects.

Adult Attachments

The capacities of parents and other caregivers for attachment are based upon the history of their relationships with their own care providers and significant others. Some parents have secure styles of attachment developed in infancy and childhood and maintained over their lifetimes. Such adults establish secure relationships with their own children in most cases, except when other issues such as unavoidable traumas occur or when children have neurobiological issues.

Many parents have histories of stress and trauma that affect their capacities for attachment. The term *resolved* is used to describe parents who have coped with, adapted to, and overcome their own adversities and trauma in their own lives. They acknowledge the difficulties they have had, recognize its affects on their development, and manage the effects.

Such parents are able to establish secure relationships with their own children. Typically parents with resolves attachment styles have had successful therapy and have also established long-term relationships of trust with a spouse or significant other. Both secure and resolved parents seek support and guidance when they experience difficulties in their relationships with their children.

Secure and resolved parents also support and guide children's explorations of the world, their developing skills, and their development of autonomy. They are available when children need them, but they allow children to explore and learn on their own terms. They are attuned and empathic over time.

Parents with histories of untreated trauma typically are inconsistent in their attunements to their children, and they establish various types of insecure attachments with their own children.

Parents with dismissive attachment styles do not acknowledge their own past traumas and hurts. They may idealize their childhoods and create a kind of fantasy for themselves. Others may acknowledge that they had some difficulties, but they tell themselves and others that their own problematic experiences have had little if any affect on them.

In turn, they do not acknowledge stresses and traumas that their children undergo. For instance, if their children have been sexually abused, dismissive parents may not recognize the necessity of helping children deal with the resulting issues. They believe variations of "I was sexually abused as a child. I'm fine. My child will be fine." They show a failure of empathy for themselves and others, including their own children.

Some dismissive parents appear to over-regulate their own emotions and can be thought of as distant parents with rigid boundaries between themselves and others, including their children. Emotional distance and disconnection are normal for them because of their own attachment histories. They bring this distance and disconnection to their relationships with others, including their own children.

When parents have preoccupied styles of attachments, they are self-focused, reliving their stresses and traumas without being able to regulate them, at least during times of stress. Unfortunately, some preoccupied parents are in continual states of stress. Such parents may shift their preoccupations to their children, becoming intrusive and overly concerned about children's well-being, to the point where they tell children how they should feel and think. They may force their meanings of events onto their children.

In brief, preoccupied parents do not allow children the autonomy children require to develop executive and self-regulatory skills. Unlike secure and resolved parents, they do not gradually relinquish their control so children can develop skills and capacities that help them to become autonomous but yet emotionally connected individuals.

In their intrusiveness and preoccupation, they usually are not attuned to their children. Under some conditions, however, they can be attuned and can allow children to think and feel on their own. Children then may have ambivalent responses to their parents, not knowing what to expect because their parents are unpredictable.

Some parents have disorganized styles of attachment that they bring into their relationships with their children. They show a range of behaviors in what appears to be random order. They may be preoccupied with their own issues at one moment, preoccupied with their children at another, dismissive of children's issues including not being aware that children are in danger, dismissive of their own issues, angry, withdrawn, and agitated. Such parents have difficulty with self-regulation, which in turn affects children's capacities for self-regulation. Under these conditions, children are confused and show disorganized, dysregulated behaviors themselves.

The following is an example of an account a woman gave of why child protection removed her children from her care three years earlier. She provides a good example of parental disorganization and issues with self-regulation. Not only it is difficult to make sense of her narrative, which is characteristic of disorganized attachments, but it appears that she did not understand that the children's behaviors were inappropriate. The children ranged in age from fourteen to four. Enid was the oldest child and Phyllis was the youngest.

You know like, we went through a tornado three years ago, and so we were stuck in a hotel room. The kids were going swimming, and they came back and they were horsing around naked, because, there's only two showers at a time, and I was trying to find a place to live, and Enid kind of hit the roof and I think Enid's reaction made an impression on Phyllis. More than anything they were doing, because I was right like, in the little. [She does not finish the sentence.]. I don't think too much could have been going on, but Phyllis talked about it at pre-school, so they had to report it.

[Question: The kids being naked, you mean?]

Yeah, well, I think she more talked about how Enid—Enid thought it was really bad that we were naked and under the sheets together. And you know, we had to talk about boundaries. And it was certainly not something I condoned, but I didn't think it was—I mean we just lost—the tornado destroyed primarily the kids' floor. They just lost everything they had, and if they were going to find some self-comfort in their bodies, I was kind of ok with that.

This mother was an untreated father incest survivor who did not believe the incest harmed her in any way. She never sought therapy and resisted it when child protection made it part of her case plan. The incest lasted from early childhood until she left home at eighteen. It is little wonder that she developed a disorganized attachment style and that she could not only not self-regulated but that she was unable to be the executive in her family. Not recognizing the inappropriateness of these behaviors suggests a major issue with her judgment, an executive function.

In summary, parent-child attachment styles mirror adult attachment styles. Adult secure and resolves styles are associated with secure parent-child attachment styles. Adult dismissive attachment styles are associated with avoidant parent-child attachment styles. Preoccupied attachment styles are associated with ambivalent parent-child attachments. Disorganized adult attachments are associated with disorganized and disordered child-adult attachments.

Attachment styles are foundational to the formation of inner working models (IWM), which are internalized expectations about self, others, and how the world works, how to behave in the world, and the meanings of human actions and events. IWMs are encoded in brain circuits. IWMs are ready to be activated depending on individuals' perceptions of events. IWMs can be thought of as cognitive maps, schemas, tapes, and inner representations. In the NEATS assessment, I use the terms IWMs and schemas interchangeably.

Over time, there are increasing numbers of sources of the components of schemas. Human beings are born with rudimentary or primary schemas such as sucking, crying, and other neurophysiological responses. Brain circuits become increasingly complex as individuals experience cognitive, emotional, and social developmental processes. For example, the capacities of a three year-old are vastly different from those of a ten year-old because of maturation of brain structures and functions, as well as maturation of other areas of developmental, such as cognitive, behavioral, emotional, and sexual.

IWMs build on each other. Children with secure attachment relationships have schemas that lead them to experience other people as safe, predictable, responsive to what they want and need and themselves as efficacious, loveable, and safe to be around. Children with secure attachments tend to evoke positive responses in others. Secure attachments thus set off feedback loops where success builds on success.

Children with insecure attachments may be confused and ambivalent about others. Some, especially those with dismissive, distant parents, may develop rigid expectations. They could be quite confident in their beliefs about themselves, others, and how the world works. For example, they may believe that antisocial behaviors are appropriate responses to perceived or actual slights or as means to get what they want.

Persons with insecure attachments could have good executive skills in some situations, but they are more prone than persons with secure attachment styles to behave in harmful or inappropriate ways. Under stress, persons with secure attachments can temporarily show poor executive and self-regulation skills.

Observations of caregivers and children are ideal for assessing quality of attachment. Signs of secure attachments include children's use of care providers as a secure base from which to explore the environment and to which to return in times of stress, mutuality and reciprocity in care provider-child interactions, and contingent responsiveness which means that the parent calibrates responses to children according to child readiness to receive parental engagements, sadness at separation, and joy at reunion.

As infants develop into toddlerhood and beyond, parents of securely attached children also structure children's environments to provide them with opportunities to challenge themselves and to develop new capacities. They allow children to attempt new tasks on their own and will show children how to perform tasks when children appear to require some guidance and are ready for their assistance. This is yet another manifestation of contingent responsiveness.

Throughout childhood and adolescents, securely attached parents provide love, warmth, safety, structure, and clear expectations. For example, a family quality associated with well-functioning teenagers is parental supervision of children's whereabouts and clear expectations for when children are at home.

Services that Promote Attachment

Interventions meant to promote secure attachments include both parents and children. Such programs will have support and educational groups for parents, structured play groups for children, and activities that include both parents and children. In addition, home visiting is an important part of attachment promotion programs. To the extent possible, these programs involve fathers as well as mothers in their educational and support efforts.

Often, principles of infant mental health are part of these programs, where the operating principle is support, education, and even therapy for parents as foundational to optimal child development.

The programs also have well-established collaborations with medical, mental health, preschools, and child care, among others. Many of these programs are part of university-based programs that combine service and research.

"Holding" and "re-birthing" programs have discredited as methods of promoting secure attachments. They are based upon misuse of research on attachment and have led to several deaths. It is best to confer with licensed professionals to identify reputable and effective programs that promote secure attachments.

Practice Note

Observations of parent and child interactions as well as conversations with parents and children provide information on styles of attachment. In Jack's case, practitioners would observe how his parents manage Jack's executive skills issues, which he would have because he has ADHD. Questions to consider include whether six year-old Jack behaves as if his parents serve as a secure base for him, whether they supervise him while at the same time allow him to experiment with new tasks on his own, and whether they help him structure his time so he completes tasks expected of a child his age.

Other questions are whether they help him manage his behaviors, understand when he has done something well, and praise him when he has behaved appropriately. There are many other attachment related behaviors that require assessment, but these are some important ones.

Parental executive function issues are interlaced with capacities for secure attachment. Parents with executive function issues may not be able to provide consistent, responsive, contingent caregiving. They require education about parenting and child development. If they are dismissive or preoccupied with their own issues, they also require professional help in order to parent effectively.

5

Trauma

Trauma is an event that is life-threatening or psychologically devastating to the point where persons' capacities to cope are overwhelmed. Any number of events may be traumatizing, including abuse and neglect, witnessing violence, death or other kind of loss of parents or siblings, abductions, car accidents, plane crashes, earthquakes, tidal waves, social dislocation, and war. Following trauma, individuals relive the traumatic event, fragmented memories related to the trauma arise unexpectedly, cognitive, emotional, and behavioral dysregulation occurs, and there is avoidance of reminders of the event. Trauma may change brain structures and become encoded in brain circuits related to memory and emotion.

Trauma and Neurobiology

Traumatic responses are expectable to extraordinary, overwhelming events. A kind of "hot button" or trigger becomes encoded in the emotion centers of the brain. Schemas can be reactivated when persons experience reminders of the original trauma. Reminders can involve any of the five senses. An example is nine-month old child who screams when he sees a woman with blonde hair because a social worker with blonde hair took him from his biological family into foster care. When hot buttons are triggered, children are at risk to dysregulate; that is, to relive the trauma. In fact, teenagers and adults, as well as children, are at risk to dysregulate when traumas are triggered.

In relation to neurobiology, the hippocampus, a pair of banana-shaped structure located on each side of the midbrain, is an important storage point for traumatic memories. The hippocampus not only stores the traumatic event itself but also the context of the traumatic event. Sounds, smells, and contextual details become associated with the trauma. Whenever individuals experience these reminders of the event, memories of the trauma flood into awareness. Often the memories and reminders are stored as bits and pieces. When the memories are evoked the memories themselves are fragmented.

Cortisol, a stress hormone, is released in response to trauma and the retriggering of trauma. Cortisol can damage brain cells in the hippo-campus and even kill them. Thus, some children and adults cannot remember major pieces of traumatic events, possibly because of damage to the cells of the hippocampus.

In addition, the hippocampus matures relatively late in life, per-haps into middle childhood or beyond. This accounts for the relatively few memories that individuals have of their early lives. Children who have trauma early in life, therefore, may have not memory of these events.

However, another brain structure, located near the hippocam-pus, matures quite early and can store the emotional component of trauma, though not the memories themselves. This structure is the al-mond-shaped amygdala, which also comes in pairs. Very young children who have experienced trauma may have no memory of the trauma, but the trauma is encoded in the amygdala.

When children relive trauma and become dysregulated, remind-ers of the traumatic event trigger brain circuits that by-pass the prefrontal cortex, which is the brain's seat of reasoning. Researchers call this the low road response because the response goes directly to the emotion center and does not engage higher order reasoning.

High road responses result when the brain circuits of the pre-frontal cortex are engaged and children are able to engage their executive functions; in other words they engage in rational thought, problem-solving, and consideration of alternatives. They may realize that they want to be with people who offer safe havens where they will experience comfort and reassurance. Some children, who have secure relationships, seek safe havens automatically. This is a beneficial adaptation that shows their inner working models developed through secure attachments are characterized by expectations that other people are trustworthy. Without much forethought, they automatically seek people they trust. They expect reassurance and kindness.

Without the engagement of reasoning, children are on automatic. Whatever is encoded in the emotion circuits will be activated. Children with histories of witnessing violence or of being victims of abuse and neglect are at high risk to respond inappropriately, including antisocially and self-destructively. Chronic repeated exposure to trauma is often called complex trauma. Children with histories of consistently secure attachments will respond in prosocial ways.

Parents as Source of Trauma

For many children, parents are the sources of their trauma. The very persons to whom children turn for safety and love are the sources of overwhelming fear and mistrust. This sets up conflicts in children that cannot be resolved without competent intervention.

Children who have witnessed domestic violence often have these responses to parents. They may seek contact with parents who have been victimized, but show a great deal of fear and avoidance because the parents remind them of the violence that traumatized them. They may be fearful of aggressor parents and avoid them, while at the same time want assurance that the aggressors will not hurt them. Children who have these circumstances can be thought of as showing ambivalent attachment styles related to trauma.

Parents who have been victimized and parents who victimize may be so preoccupied with their own issues that they are unresponsive to their children's trauma. In addition, they could have avoidant styles of attachment that lead them to minimize the effects. Domestic violence has complex effects of children, but it is a source of trauma.

Because parents in domestic violence situations typically cannot help their children to cope with the trauma, children and their parents require safety and opportunity to work through the effects of trauma. Sadly, their services often are unavailable. The trauma creates what can be a permanent disconnection between parents and children because of lack of opportunity for repair.

Parents and other adults are key to helping children work through and manage the effects of trauma. This requires direct and supportive interventions to help children deal with the trauma and build new neural circuits that lead to high-road responses, or responses that engage reasoning and are not harmful to the children and other people.

The effects of trauma can only be worked through in the safety of secure relationships. Children with histories of secure attachments, good executive skills, and relatively resilient brain structures may be more likely to seek and use help when traumatized and more likely to seek and use help when effects of trauma are triggered. Such children develop capacities to cope with, adapt to, and overcome the effects of trauma and other stressors. They, therefore, show resilience.

Children with histories of insecure attachments, compromised executive skills, and vulnerable brain structures may cope in avoidant, ambivalent, disorganized, and disordered ways. Parents of insecurely attached children may be unavailable psychologically or they may reject children's bids for help. Through experience, insecurely attached children have learned that adults are not consistently trustworthy, or they may not believe parents care, or they do not want to upset parents. Such children may have few capacities for coping with, adapting to or overcoming adversities. They often are not resilient, but react in disorganized, self-destructive, self-defeating, and sometimes antisocial ways when they experience stress and trauma.

Children with reactive attachment disorders are so fearful of attachment figures that they are unlikely to seek help and will express the effects of trauma through their behaviors which can be withdrawn, aggressive, and otherwise inappropriate.

School age and older children may make seek peers as confidants. Some peers can be helpful, but others are not. They also may seek other adults besides their parents for help with trauma-related issues. Examples of trauma where children seek help outside of their families are child sexual abuse, physical abuse, and partner violence, including physical and psychological abuse.

Children, especially those with multiple, complex traumas, may have prolonged episodes of dysregulation when traumas are triggered. They may need to scream and cry for hours when they relive trauma. The origins of trauma are important to understand so that appropriate interventions can be tailored to children's situations.

Children become dysregulated when they re-experience trauma. Parents, teachers, others may mistake dysregulation as oppositional behaviors. Persons involved with children who have experienced trauma require a great deal of psychoeducation. Most of all, parents and professionals must engage their higher order reasoning, take the high road, and not let themselves be triggered by what could be extreme child behaviors.

When children are reliving trauma, they must be made safe and precautions must be taken to ensure the safety of others. The children should not be left alone but a caring adult must be present, sometimes softly describing the child's behaviors, but overall allowing the emotions to take their course.

Once children become re-regulated, adults can talk to children about what triggered these responses. For some children, simply re-integrating them into family or school activates is all they can handle. With sensitivity and consultation, adults can make judgments about the timing of verbal processing of trauma.

Eventually children who experience such responses will learn positive ways of coping when their traumas are triggered. Compassionate responses help traumatized children develop new executive skills to manage their dysregulated behaviors. Children who have experienced trauma require parents and other adults who are psychologically and physically available to them. Adults must be able to manage their own traumas, which can be triggered when dealing with children who have experienced trauma.

Parents may require their own therapy, and they often require a great deal of instrumental, social, and emotional support and encouragement. Dealing with traumatized children is difficult. When children have neurological issues that predispose them to dysregulation, their responses to trauma may lead to a high degree of dysregulation.

Older children may want to express themselves in words and benefit when attachment figures help them to understand complex emotions and complex social interactions that give rise to powerful emotions.

In summary, trauma brings out complex issues that require intervention not only with the affected children but with the adults who are entrusted with their care. Children have every hope of developing capacities for resilience if they process adversities within the safety of secure relationships.

Practice Note

Trauma does not go away on its own, but must be dealt with directly within relationships where children feel safe. Thus, secure attachments must be established for children to process and manage trauma. As a general principle, a goal in trauma work is to help children develop high road response so that when their traumas are triggered, they immediately engage their executive skills. High road responses are characteristic of resilience.

If six year-old Jack experiences trauma, he quickly appraises his parents' trustworthiness and whether they can ensure his safety. If he decides no, he will remain silent or talk to someone he thinks is trustworthy. If his parents have issues with executive functions independent of Jack's trauma and also have problematic attachment styles, they will be unable to respond to Jack effectively and consistently. They may dismiss the effects of the trauma, believe it has gone away if he is not showing direct signs of trauma, or they may become preoccupied. However, even parents with a history of secure or resolved attachments and excellent executive skills may require psychoeducation and emotional support in order to respond effectively.

van der Kolk who has done clinical work and research with child, teens, and adults who have experienced trauma recommends that children first learn techniques of self-regulation before professionals attempt to help children to work through trauma. Meditation, yoga, vigorous exercise, finding someone to talk to are examples of the many different ways that children can learn to deal with dysregulation or to offset it.

In brief, when children have experienced trauma, a first line of professional action is to assess parents' capacities for sensitive, compassionate responses and then work out a case plan.

Self-Regulation

S elf-regulation is defined as capacities to manage and make sense of one's own thoughts, emotions, and behaviors in times of stress and in the course of everyday life. Self-regulation is often considered part of executive functions, but because of its centrality for children with behavioral issues, the NEATS assessment treats self-regulation as it own category. Capacities for self-regulation are both genetic and experiential in origin. Subjectively, children experience dysregulation as a loss of control, of unmanageability of thoughts, emotions, and behaviors. Heart rate and breathing may become accelerated.

When dysregulated, individuals throughout the life course may become fearful, anxious, withdrawn, depressed, hyperactive, lethargic, and experience emotional outbursts, bed wetting, sleep disturbances, and oppositional behaviors. Some individuals are euphoric while in dysregulated states. Dysregulation typically is painful and persons seek to re-regulate as a means of managing the emotional pain.

Self-Regulation as Process

Children learn to self-regulate through contingent, responsive parenting that begins at birth. Learning to self-regulate is a process. When infants cry and give other cues that something is wrong, they are in a state of dysregulation. As shown in chapter 4 on attachment, sensitive, responsive parents run through mental lists of possible causes such as hunger, fear, pain, desire for touch and interaction, or the need for a diaper change. When parents take care of the causes of distress, infants feel soothed, or they become re-regulated. Parents, too, feel satisfaction at being able to soothe their infants and take pleasure in the children's pleasure. Infants in these situations learn that their actions affect parents' actions and the results are mutual satisfaction.

Infants also participate in mutual, reciprocal relationships with their parents when parents respond to infants' cues about when they want interaction and when they want to stop. Cooing, talking, and playing patty cake are fun for both parents and children. After a while, children may want a rest from the interaction. They cue parents by looking away and being less responsive. Sensitive parents respect infants' desire for quiet time. Infants experience their requests as important and respected. They learn that their wishes count, and they count.

After multiple repetitions, this regulation, dysregulation, and re-regulation cycle, infants develop inner of working models of self-regulation that includes capacities to self-soothe. These self-soothing capacities become more sophisticated as children grow older. Children develop a wide range of ways to self-soothe and re-regulate. The basics develop in infancy, through contingent, sensitive responsiveness.

As discussed in chapter 4 on attachment, self-regulation develops through reciprocal, attuned relationships with parents and is an example of the external to internal to external principle in child development. Children internalize their experiences, which are encoded in brain circuits and become part of inner working models of self, others, and how the world works.

Dysregulation is common in childhood. Temper tantrums are examples. Parents and other adults help infants and young children re-regulate when they have tantrums. Children eventually develop internalized capacities for self-regulation in response to sensitive, contingent caregiver characteristic of secure relationships.

Children with insecure attachments have a much harder time with self-regulation because parents and other adults have not consistently provided the soothing, comfort, and structure necessary for internalization of capacities for self-regulation. In addition, these children may not trust adults to help them manage their strong emotions. Indeed, parental behaviors may be so stressful to children that the children dysregulate and parents are unwilling or unable to soothe them and help them to re-regulate.

Four General Styles of Self-Regulation

When children and persons of whatever age are under stress, they seek to re-regulate which is to get themselves back on an even keel. Schemas that activate themselves in response to stress and trauma can be of four general types: prosocial, antisocial, self-destructive, and inappropriate. Some children may show two or more of these styles of coping with dysregulation. The embedded particular patterns are, the more dominant one style of coping will be.

Prosocial responses at their core are secure attachment behaviors, where children seek safe havens that will soothe them and help them to re-regulate. How children re-regulate varies with their experience and development. Young children may soothe themselves through thumb-sucking and seeking a soft toy or blanket. They may want to cuddle.

Older children may also seek attachment figures, but want to talk about what happened and to work out strategies for dealing with situations that triggered the dysregulation. Physical exercise, meditation on something pleasant, drawing, and writing out feelings are some of many different strategies that can contribute to prosocial self-regulation. Children who engage in prosocial ways of dealing with stress and trauma and re-regulate are said to show resilience.

When schemas are associated with **antisocial, inappropriate, or self-destructive behaviors,** it becomes important to become aware of expectations, assumptions, and behavioral guidelines that children have internalized and to figure out how help children to redirect and manage behaviors, thoughts, and emotions, associated with particular inner working models.

Children raised in environments where violence is normative are at risk to act out their dysregulation anti-social ways such as defiance, aggression toward others, and destruction of property. Children raised in avoidant, repressive environments may react to their dysregulation through self-destructive actions, such as cutting, using chemicals, and over-eating.

Inappropriate behaviors include being unable to sit still or listen to directions. Silence and "stuffing" emotions may be attempts at self-regulation or re-regulation. Sexual acting out can be attempts at re-regulation. Children with these responses believe that parents or other adults cannot or will not help them cope with their dysregulation. Sometimes children, especially boys, learn that expressions of emotions that show hurt, sadness, and loss and "sissy" or "gay." In order to be real boys and men, they must not admit to these emotions. Figure 3 shows pathways toward prosocial, antisocial, self-destructive, and inappropriate responses to stress and trauma.

Some inner working models, formed during times of stress and trauma remain in their original undifferentiated state. They may sit inactivated for years within brain circuits but may re-activate when individuals perceive themselves to be in situations similar to those that led to their formation in the first place.

Children also learn strategies of self-regulation, dysregulation, and re-regulation through observing parents, siblings, peers, and others with whom they identify, including fictional characters in stories, films, video games, and cartoons. Strategies of self-regulation are linked to family traditions, culture, gender, and age. Gender is significant in how children manage their emotions. Girls are encouraged to express a range of emotions, while boys are permitted far fewer.

Figure 3
Trigger Events, Dysregulation, & Attempts at Re-Regulation

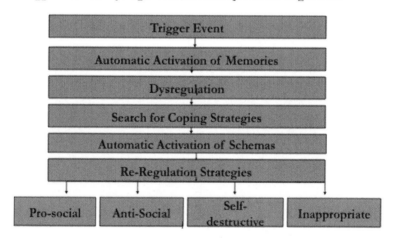

The triggers of an episode of dysregulation can puzzle adults but make sense once adults know children's histories. For example, Terrell tore up the waiting room of a child and family therapy agency. His therapist had wanted some alone time with his mother who was having struggles at work. The therapist accompanied Terrel to the waiting room where his case manager was waiting for him. The case manager then left to go the washroom. "I was only gone a minute," the case manager said.

Terrell, alone in the waiting room, thought the case manager had abandoned him. He relived the trauma related to other abandonments and apparently coped through destroying property. Obviously, abandonment is a therapeutic issue for Terrell. He has learned to express himself while dysregulated through destructive behaviors. Terrell must have repeatedly witnessed other people manage powerful emotions in these destructive ways.

Adults who are uneducated about children's trauma and dysregulation may have responded in a punitive way. The case manager first assured Terrell that she was there for him. Then she helped him put the waiting room back in order. She planned to talk to him and have him role play what he will do the next time he thinks someone has left him.

Some children may show few signs of dysregulation. Quiet children, whether girls or boys, may mask episodes of dysregulation by being quiet and withdrawn. This, however, does not mean that they have worked through the effects of trauma. They too require the safety of secure relationships to do so.

Helping Children to Self-Regulate

Children can learn to self-regulate when the adults in the various settings in which children participate know how to respond and how to guide them. Typical interventions that lead to self-regulation include sensitive, contingent responses to episodes of dysregulation that include the assurance of safety, permission to dysregulate while ensuring the safety of self, others, and property, and problem solving and empathy once the dysregulated episode is concluded.

As with other executive function issues, children with self-regulation challenges require safe, structured, predictable environments, clear expectations, and praise for any self-regulation capacities that they show. Parents of children with dysregulation issues will benefit from support groups and psychoeducation.

Some children may be unable to re-regulate stress reactions under some conditions. Children with certain neurological conditions, such as some forms of autism spectrum disorders, fetal alcohol effects, and bipolar disorders may be at high risk to dysregulate despite optimal care. What is clear that unattended trauma in the lives of children who already have such neurological issues increase he likelihood of difficulties with self-regulation. In fact, unattended trauma with or without neurological issues puts children at high risk to have issues with self-regulations. Medication, in combination with a range of other interventions, as discussed in chapter 12 on case planning, may help children with challenges related to self-regulation.

If parents have difficulties with self-regulation themselves, they and their families will benefit from therapy and perhaps self-help groups. Parents with chemical dependency and mental health issues may have particular difficulties with self-regulation, which limits their capacities to helpful with the children's self-regulation.

Professionals, such as teachers and social workers, also must educate themselves about issues related to self-regulation and dysregulation and provide themselves with the support and practice guidelines they need to be helpful to children. If they find that their personal responses interfere with their effectiveness, then therapy might benefit them.

Summary

Self-regulation is one of the executive skills. Children under the care of social services often have serious issues with self-regulation. Thus, in the NEATS assessment, self-regulation is a separate category.

Capacities for self-regulation are both genetic and environmental in origin. Children with histories of abuse and neglect, inadequate care, and trauma or who have parents who do not model self-regulation and do not help children to achieve it, are at high risk to have difficulties with self-regulation. Interventions that are effective in helping children learn to self-regulate must include both the children and the adults, such as parents, teachers, and others who have responsibility for the care of children with self-regulation issues.

Practice Note

When children have issues with self-regulation, it is important to assess parents for their self-regulation capacities. Children develop optimal self-regulation in the natural course of events in parent-child attachment relationship, in response to parental structure and guidelines, and through observing how parents self-regulate. Issues that children have with self-regulation often find their mirror images in how parents regulate themselves.

A NEATS assessment leads to comprehensive case plans. Guidelines for effective case planning are in chapter 12 When parents are willing to do whatever it takes to foster their children's healthy development and when appropriate services are available, there is reason to hope that children will reach their potential and live full and satisfying lives. Even when services are in place and parents are doing their best, however, some children experience outcomes that no one wants, such as incapacities to live independently, to anticipate the consequences of unprotected sex, or to self-regulate when traumas are triggered.

All too often, services are inadequate and parents are unable to be physically and psychologically available to their children. Many children who grow up in these circumstances still manage to live full and satisfying lives, through great effort and perhaps good luck. Someone or several people step in and are there for them.

Optimal child outcomes are reasons to cheer. Less than optimal outcomes are reasons to figure out what went wrong and what can be done to make things right for children and their families.

7

Applications:
A Case Study of Pete, 10, and his Family[1]

This chapter shows how to uses the NEATS to assess a child and his family. The assessment is organized using the five categories of the NEATS and includes the focal child as well as other family members and systems that affect the child and his family. First I present the case study and then I present the assessment itself, followed by the recommendations that are part of a case plan.

Pete is a 10 year-old boy who has trouble with regulating his moods and behaviors. Although his behaviors have changed in the past two years, he has an eight-year history of serious behavior problems. His behaviors have been so potentially harmful to himself and others that he had been placed in a psychiatric hospital two times, once at age five and a second time at age eight. His parents, Patrice and Larry, had divorced when Pete was two. Patrice had sole custody, and Larry paid child support but rarely saw his son.

The behaviors that led to Pete's second hospitalization included several episodes of aggression in school and at home that included throwing chairs and desks at teachers and other students, throwing and breaking a computer, threatening his mother Patrice with a knife, fighting with other children, and grabbing the breats and buttocks of three different girls. At times, he was silent and withdrawn, refusing to respond to other people. He swore, kicked, screamed, and threatened others when they tried to interact with him when he wanted to be left alone. He had

---

[1] Danette Jones contributed to this analysis. Names and other identifying information in this case study have been changed.

been on medication for mood issues for three years, but the medication appeared not be helping.

During the second hospitalization, Pete's psychiatrist said he showed a disorganized attachment style that resulted from what appeared to be complex traumas that he experienced over several years. The psychiatrist noted that Patrice's behaviors had traumatized Pete and that she had been unable to provide the safety and security that Pete required to work through his traumas, and that she. Further, the psychiatrist said, Pete's father Larry had failed to provide a secure base and by his absence had contributed to Pete's issues with unattended trauma. Both parents have to step up to the plate, he said.

After several sessions with Pete's parents, together and individually, the psychiatrist concluded that Larry was the more able parent and that Patrice was unable at that time to parent effectively. The psychiatrist appeared to have accepted Larry's explanation for his absence from Pete's life. Larry said he had stayed away because of a contentious relationship with Patrice and because of a cocaine addiction. When he stopped using cocaine and became active in Narcotics Anonymous, he stated that his own recovery consumed his time. He assured the psychiatrist that he wanted his son to live with him, and he was prepared to do whatever it took to do right by his son. He had been clean and sober for two years.

Larry Awarded Custody

Larry then petitioned the court for full custody of Pete. Based on the recommendation of Pete's psychiatrist, the judge awarded custody to Larry and ordered supervised visits between Pete and Patrice every other week for two hours at a child visitation center. A child visitation center is set up so that the custodial parent brings the children in one door and leaves the children under the supervision of a professional. The parent then exists through the same door. The non-custodial parent enters another door about ten minutes later. The parents do not see each other. The visitation room is child friendly, with toys, games, computers, and child-size furniture. One or more professionals supervise the visits from a respectful distance, writing notes on the interactions between parents and children.

Patrice vowed to appeal the court decision, but she did not. Patrice is inconsistent in showing up for her visits. At first, Pete would have tantrums, throw things, and be inconsolable when she did not appear. After several months of her inconsistent visiting, Pete became more accepting of not being able to count on her.

The two years Pete has lived with his father have been the most stable of his life. He has made progress is self-regulation and executive skills. He now pays attention in class, is respectful to other students and to teachers, and complies with school rules. He is mainstreamed in math, science, and gym, while previously all of his classes were in settings for children with emotional and behavioral issues. He has earned As and Bs in school. Earlier in his life, he received Cs, Ds, and Fs.

Patrice's Background

When Pete lived with his mother Patrice, she had periods when she appeared to be loving and sensitive. She also flew into rages, or withdrew and gave Pete the silent treatment. Rather than foster a healthy relationship between Pete and his father, Patrice made critical remarks and accusations of extreme cruelty, which Pete never witnessed, but he could neither refute nor confirm her reports. This left Pete confused about his father and stressed when his father stopped seeing him. Patrice complained that Larry did not pay child support, when in fact he did, according to court documents.

Patrice appears to have agoraphobia, which is an anxiety disorder characterized by fear of leaving familiar places, such as the home. She works at home as a website designer. She reported that she has had an eating disorder since her early teens, characterized by binge eating and then vomiting. This may be partially neurobiological in origin. While a student at a college of art and design, she stole money from dormitory classmates and was expelled. Given the instability of her moods, she may have a mild form of bipolar disorder, called cyclothymia, but she has not wanted to get a psychiatric diagnosis. She said her uncle sexually abused her when she was between the ages of five and ten, and she participated in a girls' group for sexual abuse. She believes the sexual abuse has had no effect on her and in fact has made her a stronger person.

Patrice appears to have high intelligence. She had top grades while in college. She worked for a software company for three years and made a lot of money. She met Larry a year after she left college. They married a year later. Pete was born two years after their marriage. Patrice may have had post-partum depression because Larry reported that after Pete's birth, Patrice was never the same. She alternated between despondency and rage. She did not return to her job at the software company. She had earned enough money to have a large savings account.

Patrice worked sporadically in the software field after her divorce from Larry, but she quit or was fired several times for emotional outbursts. While employed most recently, she threatened to throw scissors at her boss who fired her on the spot.

Patrice was an excellent housekeeper. Her home was well-organized and spotless, and she kept Pete on a strict schedule of meals and bedtime. In this one area, she was predictable. Pete was meticulously clean, and she dressed him in the latest fashions. Both she and Pete took pride in their appearance.

Neither parent remarried, although Patrice has lived with several men since the divorce. Pete reported that these men often beat his mother and sometimes beat him. He saw his mother defend herself with a kitchen knife several times. Pete denied that any of the man sexually abused him, but his sexual harassment of other children suggests that he may have experienced sexual trauma.

Larry's Background

Larry has had a long-term relationship with a woman, but they do not live together. Larry said he wants to keep his life simple until Pete is older and shows long-term stability.

Larry had been a cocaine addict for many years. He managed to keep his job as a financial planner while using cocaine mostly on weekends. After a prostitute whom he had spent the weekend on a cocaine binge accused him of rape, he voluntarily entered a drug treatment program, which he successfully completed. He pled no contest to the rape charge and received probation, which he served. He no longer is on paper.

He has been active in Narcotics Anonymous since that time. Larry has a hobby farm in the suburbs, and besides raising alpacas for their fiber and riding his three horses, he enjoys golf, swimming, and travel.

Effects of Parents' Behaviors on Pete

Patrice's unpredictable behaviors, criticism of Larry, erratic lifestyle with men, and Larry's virtual abandonment appear to have had serious effects on Pete's development. In addition, he witnessed verbal and physical violence and may have been sexually abused. Pete, therefore, experienced complex trauma, with no secure attachments with which to work out the effects of the trauma.

In addition, Pete may have a genetic predisposition to dysregulate, passed down possibly from his parents. His father's cocaine addiction could have resulted from issues with self-regulation. His use of cocaine could have been a means of re-regulation. Patrice's bulimia, agoraphobia, and issues with self-regulation may be possibly genetic in origin but could also be related to the effects of child sexual abuse and other trauma that she has not disclosed.

Larry Sees the Extent of Pete's Issues

When Pete moved in with him, Larry had been sober for two years and stated that he was ready and eager to be a full-time father. He complied with the aftercare requirements involved with Pete's second hospitalization, but he did not believe that Pete's behaviors were challenging. "All he needs is love," Larry said. "I've got plenty of that for my boy."

Once aftercare was completed, Larry sought no more services. He asked the psychiatrist to take Pete off medication, which he did, although he recommended a slow tapering off. Larry said he did as the psychiatrist asked. Larry continued to participate in Narcotics Anonymous two times a week. Pete participated in the children's group.

A month after Pete moved in, Larry contacted the social worker at the psychiatric hospital, distraught with Pete's behaviors. He had gotten into fights in school and had run out of the classroom and hid several times. He continually argued with his father about bedtime, household chores, and helping around the farm. He struck his father with his hand one time. Larry realized that he and Pete required supportive services. The social worker set up an appointment with Pete's psychiatrist.

Larry consulted with the psychiatrist the next day. He said he still prefers that Pete not be medicated, but that he is now willing to get involved in services. The psychiatrist outlined a treatment plan, and the social worker helped Larry with follow-through.

The next week, Pete began weekly individual and group therapy at the local mental health center. Larry participated fully in the treatment. Father and son began family therapy at the center every other week. Larry also participated in a support group for parents of children with special needs. Larry exchanged respite care with two other families so that he could take time to travel for his job. Through these many services, Larry learned the importance of consistency, structure, and authoritative parenting. Pete did not go back on medication. He seemed to thrive when he knew what Larry expected of him.

Pete and Larry have been heavily involved in multiple services for almost two years. Gradually, Pete's aggressive outbursts and angry withdrawal episodes decreased to now being rare. When stressed, Pete engages in a variety of prosocial and appropriate responses that include talking things over with his father and therapists, practicing appropriate means of self-regulation in therapy sessions, and using physical exercises, especially farm chores, to help him reduce his stress levels.

In summary, Pete is a 10 year-old boy with issues related attachment, self-regulation, and trauma. For six years, his mother parented him by herself. She was unable to provide the stability and security that Pete and all children require to thrive. His father, too, had similar issues, but he showed a willingness and capacities for dealing with them. Pete has lived with his father for two years, father and son have participated in intensive services, and Pete's behaviors and capacities in all domains have improved.

The following is an application of the NEATS assessment to Pete and his family. This analysis contains information that is not in the above case summary.

N (Neurobiology)

- All family members are of average or above average intelligence.
- Pete has easily triggered hot buttons that appear to have been encoded in his brain circuitry as schemas or inner working models (IWMs) that bypass the prefrontal cortex. He has emotional-behavioral responses that are disengaged from executive functions.
- Pete may have neurological issues that were transmitted genetically.
- Pete is no longer on medication. The stability he has experienced since he began living with his father appears to be reflected in more balanced neurological functioning.
- Patrice has no psychiatric diagnoses but have never consulted a psychiatrist. She appears to have bulimia and agoraphobia, both of which can be partially or wholly neurological in origin. She may have suffered post-partum depression and has unpredictable mood swings.
- Larry may also have neurological issues that led him to use cocaine as a mood stimulant and/or to self-medicate.

E (Executive Function)

- In the past, Pete had issues with attention, rule following, impulsivity, anticipation of consequences, planning, and problem-solving. His classroom behaviors and behaviors at home and in the community have much improved since he began living with his father.
- Patrice had issues with executive function as well, as she did not seem to understand how her behaviors affected Pete. In addition, she brought violent, possibly sexually abusive men into their home. She also saw no reason to get professional help for Pete's well-being and her own.
- Larry showed poor executive skills when he rarely saw Pete while Patrice had custody.
- Larry shows capacities for flexible thinking, as shown by his change of mind about what Pete might require in order to function well. At first, he dismissed the seriousness of his son's condition, but he revised his appraisal of Pete's capacities and engaged in an array of services.

- Larry models healthy executive functions and provides the structure Pete needs to develop executive skills. Larry ensures that Pete has the therapy he requires and participates full in Pete's treatment. He and Pete participate in family therapy. He continues to attend Narcotics Anonymous and Pete attends the children's group. Larry also participates in parent psychoeducation programs and the parent support group.

A (Attachment)

- Pete may be increasing his capacities for secure attachment as a result of the stability he has experienced for the past two years with his father, in combination with the multiple services with which he has engaged with his father.
- For Pete's first eight years, his parents did not provide him with the sensitive, responsive caregiving required to provide a foundation for the development of secure attachments and the qualities that develop from secure attachments.
- In the past, Pete's inner working models (IWMs) appears to involve expectations that parental/authority figures are not only untrustworthy but threatening and unpredictable. He is learning that Larry is a secure base who provides the sensitive, responsiveness and contingent disciple that children require.
- Pete does not view Patrice as a safe haven where he can find comfort and understanding when he is about to dysregulate. When he lived with her, he acted out in antisocial ways, by destroying property, threatening to hurt others, and engaging in inappropriate behaviors.
- Patrice appears to have a disorganized attachment style. She was inconsistent in her care and in many ways psychologically unavailable. Pete was exposed to his mother's unpredictable emotions and behaviors. She was unable to soothe him and foster re-regulation of his aroused states. He has struggled with learning to think before he acts and to self-regulate.
- Pete also appears to have a disorganized attachment style, which, not surprisingly, reflects his mother's. He could have experienced multiple traumas, of which social service providers have little information. Untreated trauma is associated with disorganized attachment styles.

- Patrice undermined Pete's relationship with his father and any other person she viewed as a threat. She manufactured scenarios of Larry being abusive, in order to keep Pete from his father.
- Pete's psychiatrist was so concerned about Patrice's care of Pete that he recommended supervised contact at a visitation center.
- Larry may have fostered an insecure attachment with Pete as a result of his absence from his son's life for about four years. His two-year effort to redress his mistakes are having good results for Pete.
- Larry may have some elements of a dismissive attachment style. Not only did he appear to minimize the effects of his absence on Pete, but he appeared at first to minimize the seriousness of Pete's condition. After experiencing Pete's behaviors first-hand, he became open to psychoeducation and a range of services. His willingness for these services have increased his capacities to connect to Pete, which reflects a secure adult attachment style.
- At present, Larry appears to be emotional available, consistent, and sensitively responsive to his son.

T (Trauma)

- Patrice's behaviors could have been traumatizing to Pete, as could his separations from his father. Disorganized attachment disorder is found in severely maltreated children. Patrice appears to have been a major source his attachment trauma, if attachment trauma is a good description of his condition. Pete may have also been maltreated in other ways that remain unknown to social services.
- Patrice's disorganized attachment style is likely based in unresolved childhood trauma as well as perhaps genetics—e.g., how she is "wired." She has refused to discuss her childhood and adolescence, which suggests she may have experienced trauma that is too difficult for her to discuss. Patrice may need the safety of secure relationships before she will begin to cope with, adapt to, and overcome her own traumas.
- Patrice may have had no one to help her process whatever traumas she may have experienced or to deal with changes in her life that may have led to her difficulties with self-regulation. Given her difficulties with executive function, attachment, and self-regulation, it is unlikely that the treatment she received for being a survivor of childhood sexual abuse was effective.

- Larry may have experienced trauma in his life that he may or may not have dealt with. There is no information about Larry's trauma history.
- Larry appears to have capacities to provide a secure base by which Pete may be able to process and perhaps learn to manage his trauma. Many of Pete's dysregulated low road responses have been transformed into more frequent high road responses. Pete is less likely to act out in antisocial and inappropriate ways, and more likely to seek out his father when he is stressed. Thus, Pete may be in the process of developing new IWMs that help him live a more self-regulated life.

S (Self-regulation)

- In the past, Pete attempted to re-regulate through antisocial (aggressive verbally, physically and sexually toward others), self-destructive (banging his head on the floor), and inappropriate (screaming and tantrums) methods, although with structure, warmth, and rewards he shows some capacities for self-regulation.
- In the past, Pete required psychiatric hospitalizations to become stabilized. In the two years he had lived with Larry, Pete has had no behaviors that require hospitalization.
- Since Patrice had difficulty with self-regulation, she provided neither the care nor the modeling that led to Pete's internalization of capacities for self-regulation. Pete appears to have experienced persistent distress in response to his mother's distressing behaviors. She could not help him re-regulate, and she appears to have been a source of some of his stress.
- According to Pete's psychiatrist, Patrice's disorganized behaviors sent mixed messages to Pete. These led to difficulties in forming secure IWMs of self and others, and he did not develop strong executive skills. Without these IWMs and executive skills Pete has been unable to make sense of and manage his thoughts, feelings, or behaviors. These incapacities fit the definition of dysregulation.
- Larry appears to have capacities for self-regulation, and, when he is upset, he talks things over with members of the parent support group, with therapists, or with other NA members for advice and reassurance.

Recommendations

Pete presently lives with his father Larry and has supervised visits twice a month with his mother Patrice. Though mainstreamed for three classes, he still seems to want and need special education in a small classroom where teachers provide structure, safety, and warmth.

The primary recommendation is for Pete's father Larry to continue what he has been doing for the past two years. The case plan that is in place is helpful to both father and son.

However, Pete's mother Patrice continues to be unable to be a consistent presence in Pete's life. She often does not show up for visits with Pete. While Pete appears to do well without her support, Patrice would contribute a great deal to her son's well-being and to her own by engaging with professional services. She has the financial resources for a full psychiatric and medical work-up. This would be important to do in order to identify the sources of her issues and to explore possible helpful responses. Patrice would benefit from the safety of secure professional relationships.

It is likely that the recommendations from a psychiatric or psychological work-up would include individual therapy with a focus on trauma work, a support group for women survivors of child sexual abuse, treatment for her agoraphobia, possible medication for the agoraphobia, parent education groups, and parent support groups. A longer term plan, would be to participate with Pete in family therapy sessions so that mother and son can work through the many issues that Pete now has that have resulted from her disorganized parenting. Even further down the line is a plan for post-divorce counseling between her and Larry. They have many past unresolved issues that affect their son and their own quality of life.

Once she engages in these services, she will be much more likely to be consistent in her visits with Pete. When she is with Pete, she will be more likely to be emotionally available and sensitive to him. Eventually, she may be stable enough to spend increasing amounts of unsupervised time with him.

Pete and Larry enjoy the hobby farm, but they could do with more recreational activities. Larry could resume playing golf, and, if Pete is interested, Pete could take golf lessons and play with his father. Father and son would benefit if they have one family activity a week such as golf, bowling, and water parks. Larry could also take vacations with Pete and some vacations with his long-term friend. If Patrice has stabilized, Pete could stay with her while Larry is on vacation. Pete and his friend should also go out together one night a week for an activity they both enjoy.

Patrice would also benefit from more recreational time. Until she can regulate her agoraphobia and mood issues, however, she will find this difficult. Also issues related to possible bulimia need to be clarified and responded to.

In summary, Pete is a 10 year-old boy who has made progress with issues related to self-regulation that may be partially neurobiological in origin. He also has serious issues with attachment, trauma, self-regulation, and executive function. He lived with a mother who has an eating disorder, agoraphobia, and possible other undiagnosed psychiatric conditions. He was subjected to a chaotic lifestyle that may have been resulted in a complex series of traumas that he experienced over several years. His father had little or no contact with him for about four years, creating further issues with trauma, attachment, and self-regulation. He lived with his father for the past two years and made gains in attachment, self-regulation and executive function. Pete appears to be on a favorable developmental pathway.

Applications:
A Case Study of Ian, 11, and his Family[2]

This application of the NEATS uses a different format than the previous application. In this case analysis, I apply the NEATS on the information about the case as the case unfolds. I interpret the new pieces of information through the application of the NEATS. At the end of the case study is a service plan based on the five categories of the NEATS.

Ian was seven years old when he sexually abused a three year-old boy named Annie on multiple occasions for about a year. The girl was the daughter of a neighbor who took care of Ian after school and when Ian's mother Marie had to travel on business. The abuse involved vaginal and anal penetration. The abuse took place at Ian's home and at the girl's home, out of sight of the parents who were at home at the time of the abuse. Maddie, Annie's mother, discovered the children in a state of undress and asked them what was going on. The two children told her immediately. Maddie reported the abuse to the police.

Ian was remorseful about the sexual abuse and was distraught when confronted with the allegations. He cried and said that he knew what he had done was wrong. He said, "It's not good for little kids to do that."

Maddie had provided child care to Ian since he was a toddler. After the sexual abuse came to light, Maddie talked to Ian about the abuse, assured him that did that she still loved him and did not hate him

---

[2] Sue Keskinen contributed to the writing of the case study.

52

and that she would continue to take care of him. She told him that he could never be alone with her daughter again.

The police did not charge Ian with a crime because he was too young. In the state where Ian lived, children can be charged with crimes at age 10 and older. Instead, the police made a referral to social services.

Marie, Ian's mother, told social services that she was concerned about Ian's sexual behaviors and worried that her son-in-law may have sexually abused Ian. Marie also said the abuse was not totally Ian's fault. She asked "If it was that bad, why does Maddie let Annie play with him? She still takes care of Ian. I'm not putting this all on him." Marie appeared interested in following through on referrals for a psychosexual evaluation for Ian, but she did not.

Maddie told social service professionals that Marie did not adequately supervise Ian and that she wasn't getting Ian the help he needed and wanted. She also said that Marie spends quality time with her son, especially when they play sports together.

Maddie was correct about Marie's lack of motivation to get help for her son. For three years, Marie had one reason after another for not following through on referrals for an evaluation of Ian. Marie did enroll himself and Ian in a voluntary program we will call EXCEL, which is designed to provide supportive services such as recreation and psychoeducation groups for children who have committed felony-level offenses and have other risks that place them on a developmental pathway that could lead to juvenile delinquency and correctional placements. A semivoluntary program, the parents can choose EXCEL or a child protection investigation. In this agency, case managers attempt to form relationships with the children and their parents, make appropriate referrals, and advocate for the family and children in schools, courts and other social service agencies.

The case managers, however, have no legal authority and therefore cannot petition the court to order an evaluation for Ian. Instead, Marie gave permission for Ian to participate in several different psychoeducation and recreation programs that EXCEL provided, such as groups on emotions, peer relationships, and sexual abuse prevention and trips to ball games, movies, and bowling.

In summary, Ian is a seven year-old boy who acted out sexually for about a year with a three year-old girl. His mother Marie expressed concern for her son, but also did not believe his behaviors were serious enough to warrant professional treatment. Marie, however, enrolled Ian in EXCEL, a program whose goals are to enchance child and family well-being and divert children from the juvenile and adult correctional systems.

The following is an example of using the NEATS as part of an on-going assessment. As service providers learn more about the family, the NEATS assessment is revised.

Application of the NEATS

Neurobiological: So far no information.

Attachment: Two attachment figures appear to be present in Ian's life: Maddie, who is Ian's child care provider, and Marie, Ian's mother. Maddie appears both committed and attached to Ian and appropriately concerned about Marie's parenting. Marie stated concern for her son, but did not follow through. This suggests a dismissive parenting style. So far there was no mention of Ian's father or other attachment figures.

Teachers describe Ian as shy and adorable. He interacts with other children, but in a quiet way. Other children appear to like him. He does well in drawing, math, and sports, but is having trouble with reading and social studies.

There is no information on Ian's styles of attachment to Maddie, his father, or his mother. Marie mentioned that her son-in-law may have sexually abused Ian. Ian therefore would have attachment issues with this man, probably a disorganized attachment.

Executive function: Ian appears to have issues with executive function. On the one hand, he sexually abused Annie, and on the other, he was remorseful. This suggests that he did not anticipate the consequences for himself or for Annie, whom he had known since she was born. He sexually abused Annie many times without considering what might happen as a result. His judgment was inadequate.

Marie's executive function may be impaired because she did not see that Ian needs help and that Maddie was being kind and generous. Her statement that she is not putting this all on Ian casts doubt on her understanding of what her son required in order to develop in healthy ways. Marie did not follow through on sex-specific evaluation and treatment for her son.

Maddie may have good executive skills because she continued to include Ian in her family life and closely supervised Ian when he was in her care. She was clear about how self felt about Ian, that she was still a part of his life, and that she would supervise him more closely than before.

Trauma. The response to being found out as sexually abusing a much younger child probably traumatized Ian. There is no information on trauma that Marie and Maddie may have experienced. Annie probably experienced trauma, and Maddie had obtained services for her.

Self-regulation. Ian appeared to have difficulty regulating his sexual behaviors in prosocial ways. He acted out sexually, which suggests that some powerful emotions were driving him, but he was also remorseful afterward, which suggests that he was not able to control his drive to act out.

Ian presents no behavior problems at home, school, or community. He completes his homework. Teachers think he is adorable.

Marie underplayed and perhaps under-reacted to Ian's sexual action out and the extent of his personal issues. Maddie appears to have good self-regulation. She was clear to Ian that he had done something wrong, but she informed him of her intentions in a measured, clear way, neither under-reacting or minimizing what he had done nor over-reacting.

Possible Child Neglect

Besides the concerns that Maddie expressed, other neighbors worried that Marie did not provide adequate supervision. Ian was often out at night by himself. It is the type of neighborhood where families know one another, parents keep an eye on their neighbor's kids, and kids play together in yards and on the street. Ian's family has lived in the neighborhood since before Ian was born.

Application of the NEATS

Executive Function: This lack of supervision raises questions about Marie's judgment about Ian's safety.

Attachment: Lack of supervision raises additional questions about Marie's attachment style. Her apparent inattention to Ian's physical safety is more evidence of dismissiveness.

Some Family History

Ian is a white child who lives with Marie in their own home in a middle-class neighborhood. Marie is law-abiding, has no criminal history, and no history of drug and alcohol problems. Ian's father Rick died of pancreatic cancer three years ago when Ian was four. Rick and Marie owned a sporting goods store, which Marie now runs on her own. The business provides a good income. Marie runs an organized household with regularly scheduled meals, bedtimes, homework times, and recreation. She prepares nutritious meals, and Marie keeps a clean house. Ian is neat and clean in appearance. Marie stated that she has been depressed since her husband died.

Marie's marriage to Rick was her first and Rick's second. Rick had been 14 years older than Marie and did not want more children, but he gave in to Marie's desire for a child. Marie's pregnancy with Ian was uneventful. He birth scores were high. The medical team expressed no concerns about his health.

At the time of his marriage to Marie, Rick had a daughter named Martha from his first marriage, which had ended in divorce. His ex-wife raised Martha, but Rick supported his daughter financially and saw her frequently. Rick's reluctance to become a father again changed when Ian was born. He was immediately taken with his son and spent a lot of time with him.

Both Rick and Marie were good at sports. Ian's gift from his parents at his two-year birthday included a miniature baseball glove. Father and son played a form of soccer in the backyard from the time Ian could walk. Marie and Rick introduced Ian to swimming before he was a year old through baby swimming classes. They had a membership in the Y and attended at least once a week.

Ian met his developmental milestones on time, and he had regular pediatric care. He experienced no major illness or accidents.

Application of the NEATS

Executive function. There is questionable judgment for both Marie and Rick about the wisdom of having a child when the father agrees to it only to please his wife. Rick and Marie owned a successful business, which suggests good executive function. Following Rick's death, Marie's work history and income suggest good executive function, as does her physical care of Ian and their home.

Attachment. Rick's reluctance about having another child disappeared as soon as Ian was born, suggesting that he had capacities for secure attachment. Marie wanted a child very much. Like Rick, she became an involved parent. Their family activities suggest secure attachments.

Ian appeared to be developing well, suggesting that he had secure attachments to his family.

More Family History

When Ian was almost four, Rick was diagnosed with pancreatic cancer and died within six months. Although Rick and Marie arranged child care, Ian spent a great deal of time with his father during his illness. Rick was clear about his love for Ian and expressed sadness that he had to leave him.

Marie reported that Ian's relationship with his father had been "great for a four year old" and that Ian was sad when his father died. She said that Ian wishes his father were alive and that Ian talks about his father all the time. Marie did not receive grief counseling for herself or her son after Rick's death. Marie stated that she has been depressed since Rick died.

A few months after Rick's death, Ian went on a school camping trip. Ian got homesick. One of the teachers called Marie who picked him up, stayed overnight at a motel with him, and dropped him back at the camp the next morning. The teacher said that Ian just needed a "mom fix." He was a full participant in the camping activities for the rest of the weekend.

Marie and Ian spend enjoyable time together doing sports. They love professional football, basketball, and baseball and go to a British-style pub to watch international soccer. Their favorite team is Manchester United. Marie was a three-letter athlete in high school and taught her son how to play many different sports. Ian excels in soccer and baseball. Marie is proud of her son's skills.

Application of the NEATS

Attachment: Ian appears to have had a secure attachment to his father Rick. Father and son spent a lot of time together, and their activities were mutually enjoyable. As he was dying, Rick did as much as he could to be sensitive to Ian. Ian's sadness at Rick's death and his wish that he were still alive are understandable responses. That Ian talks to Marie about his father suggests that Marie has some openness to her son's grief and could be providing the support and care that Ian needs to work through the trauma of the loss.

Ian's desire to see his mother while on a camping trip suggests that Ian has anxiety about attachments, which is understandable because his father had died so recently. Marie apparently was his secure base. Marie responded appropriately by going to the camp site and spending time with Ian. Marie did a good job of serving as a secure base.

Sports are a source of enjoyment and connection between mother and son. Marie's pride in Ian's skills is another
indicator of secure attachment.

Trauma. The loss of Rick was a major trauma for Ian
and Marie, although Rick's sensitivity to Ian might have helped
him to cope. Marie appears to have been psychologically available to Ian at least some of the time because she knew how
much Ian missed his father and she and Ian talked about him a
lot. Grief counseling may have helped mother and son cope with
and adapt to their loss of Rick.

Self-Regulation. Depression has many dimensions, and
one of them is an incapacity to regulate negative moods. Marie
stated that she has been depressed since Rick's death.

Additions to the Household

Two years after Rick died, Marie's stepdaughter Martha married
and a few months later had a baby boy she named Brian. After living on
her own with her husband Bill for three years, Martha and Brian moved
in with Marie and Ian. She had separated from Bill because of physical
and emotional abuse. She was afraid Bill would harm their son. She was
pregnant with their second child. Soon afterward, Bill moved in, too.

Their stay was supposed to be short-term, but Martha and her
family made little effort to find other housing. Bill was a drug dealer with
a series of short-term jobs that required few skills, such as dishwasher
and car wash attendant. He had one conviction for criminal sexual conduct against children aged five to nine. Ian was six and his nephew was
nephew was three when Marie added Martha, Brian, and Bill to the
household.

Application of the NEATS

Attachment: Marie might have experienced a secure attachment with her stepdaughter Martha since she allowed
Martha and her family to move in with her and Ian. She may also
have not have known how to say no. There is little information
on the quality of attachment between Marie and Martha.

Whether and how Marie prepared Ian for the changes in the household composition is unknown. Ian's style of attachment to Martha is also unknown. Her presence could have aroused anxiety about having another mother figure in the home, or awakened hope that he would have a secure attachment with her. What her pregnant state meant to him is unknown. How Ian responded to his nephew Brian and brother-in-law Bill is unknown. At first, he may have looked to Bill for a father figure.

Executive function. Marie showed poor judgment when she allowed her son-in-law Bill to move in. She should have been more cautious because she knew that he had abused Martha and Martha was afraid he would hurt Brian. Marie could have inquired about Bill's sources of income and his criminal history. Furthermore, it is unclear whether Marie had the good judgment to help Ian through these major household changes.

Trauma: These household changes could have triggered traumatic memories for Ian related to his father's death.

The Death of Brian

Shortly after Bill moved in, Martha gave birth to a second child, a daughter Jasmine. When Martha returned home from the hospital with Jasmine, she found Brian to be bruised, clingy, and anxious. She brought him to the emergency room. Child protection did an assessment, but no maltreatment was found. A few months later, Martha brought Brian to the emergency room with multiple bruises. Brian died.

Bill said Ian had killed Brian. For a while, Ian thought he had because he had thrown a toy at Brian and hit him on the chest. The police interviewed Ian to determine who killed Brian. He cried throughout the interview.

Bill was convicted of murdering Brian and received a life sentence. Besides the sexual abuse conviction mentioned earlier, while in jail on the murder conviction, Bill used a steel shank and forced another inmate to allow anal penetration and oral sex.

Marie said that Ian "reacted not real well" to Brian's death. She thought Ian "stuffed" his emotions. She stated that Ian does not talk about his nephew at all. Marie believed "the person who killed Brian may have sexually abused Ian."

Martha and her infant daughter Jasmine moved out of the home while Bill was on trial for murder. She divorced Bill and remarried. She and her family visit Ian and Marie on holidays.

Application of the NEATS

Attachment. Marie showed attunement to Ian when she described Ian's reactions to Brian's death. She also was sensitive enough to recognize the possibility that Bill may have sexually abused Ian. She would have shown even more sensitivity had she expressed concern about Ian's lack of emotion expression and silence about Brian's death.

Executive Function. That Bill's judgment was seriously impaired is without question, not only because he killed Brian but that he accused Ian of the crime.

Ian, at six years old, did not have capacities to understand that he did not kill his nephew. The accusation and the fact that he threw a toy at him was enough to make him think that he might have killed him.

There's no information about whether Marie suspected that Bill was physically abusing Brian before Brian died.

Trauma: The death of Brian was a major trauma for Ian. Bill's accusation that Ian had killed him added to the trauma. That Ian thought he might have killed him made the trauma even worse. The police interview is likely to have compounded the trauma.

Bill's conviction of sexual abuse of minors and then his rape of an inmate while in jail awaiting trial for murder show he had significant issues with abusive, violent sexual behaviors. Marie may be correct in thinking that Bill had sexually abused Ian. If so, Ian has experienced sexual trauma that would complicate previous traumas of his father's death, the death of Brian, and Bill's accusation that Ian was responsible for Brian's death. Ian probably experienced trauma when he witnessed Bill abusing Brian. When Martha and Jasmine left the home, Ian may have experienced further trauma. By age six, Ian had lived through several traumatic events.

Attachment. There is no additional information about Marie and Ian's styles of attachment to each other. There is no information about Martha's and Ian's styles of attachment with each other.

Ian's style of attachment to Brian is unclear, but his sadness indicates that his death was a significant loss. There is no information on Ian's attachment to his sister Martha, but he may have experienced her exit from the home as a loss. The same may be true of the infant Jasmine. Ian's style of attachment to Bill is unknown, but it is likely to have been ambivalent and even disorganized, given Bill's violence toward Brian and his probable sexual abuse of Ian.

Bill's inner working models (IWM), which, as discussed earlier, are assumptions, expectations, and beliefs about self, others, and how the world works, apparently permitted him to be violent toward his toddler son to the point where he killed him. This is further, rather obvious, evidence of his disorganized style of attachment. Living with such a man must have had deep effects on Ian.

Maria's dismissive attachment style could have contributed to her lack of understanding about how dangerous Bill was and how much Ian required her protection from Bill.

Self-regulation. Bill obviously did not have capacities to regulate his behaviors and emotions, or, he chose not to based on his beliefs about his own entitlements. No one may ever know what was going on with him that he beat Brian, a toddler, his son, and eventually killed him, but his is an extreme case of dysregulation or lack of self-regulation and callous disregard for the well-being of others.

Ian cried when the police questioned him about Brian's death. This is an appropriate reaction for a six year old. That he had experienced the loss of his father adds to his vulnerability. Ian did not talk to Marie about Brian's death, Bill's conviction, and the departure of Martha and Jasmine. This is further evidence to support the idea that Marie has a dismissive attachment style. Ian showed similar dismissiveness in regard to his own trauma, a result of Marie's modeling and her probable discouragement of his dealing openly with his multiple traumas.

Denial and Self-Blame

When a school social worker asked Ian who hurt his nephew, Ian responded, "No one hurt him. I don't know how he died." Ian did not want to talk about Brian's death and the circumstances around it. Maybe the social worker did not ask the right questions. When the police officer asked Ian if he blamed himself for her death, the officer said that "Ian fell apart" and admitted he believed he was to blame.

Even after this traumatic event Marie did not seek professional help for herself and her son. She said she doesn't have the two or three hours that it takes for therapy. She said he wants Ian to "move on" and doesn't want to put him through any more stress. She apparently made no effort to create conditions where Ian would feel safe enough to talk about the meanings of Brian's death.

Application of the NEATS

Executive function. Marie had the judgment to know that Ian was affected by his nephew's death, but she made no move to get psychological help and guidance for herself and her son. She also did not help Ian to deal with how Brian's death affected him. This suggests a poor executive function related to a dismissive attachment style. From her point of view, however, she was doing the best things she could for Ian.

Attachment. Marie is aware of how Ian reacted Brian's death, but she did not seem to understand how this trauma on top of the trauma of losing his father may have been more than any child could possibly handle without a lot of comfort and attention and love from a parent and, additionally, professional help.

That Ian did not talk about his nephew suggests that Marie did not know how important this is, nor did she know how to emotionally available to create conditions where Ian would feel safe enough to express her feelings and talk about what the events meant to her. Wanting Ian to move on suggests a dismissive adult attachment style.

While Ian appears to have elements of secure attachment with his mother Marie, the pattern also has elements of dismissiveness on Marie's part and avoidant on Ian's. As mentioned in chapter 4 on attachment, children's attachment styles often mirror their parents'. This is the case with Marie and Ian.

When the teacher asked Ian about fault in Brian's death, his detached apparent dismissiveness dissolved, and he cried in deep distress.

To service providers, Marie appeared primarily dismissive, refusing treatment for his son and expressing a desire to move on. Allowing Ian to participate in EXCEL indicates some capacities for recognition of the difficulties that Ian had experienced.

Trauma. It was soon after Brian's death that Ian began to act out sexually with Annie, who, when the abuse began, was two years old. There could be a connection between the sexual acting out and these recent traumas. Ian did not have a safe haven where he could work out the effects of these recent traumas and the loss of his father.

Ian's crying when the teacher asked him about fault in Brian's and then declaring he was at fault suggested unattended trauma.

Self-regulation. Ian and Marie avoid expressing their feelings, neither acting out in anti-social ways nor being self-destructive. With the degree of trauma that both mother and son had suffered, the avoidant and dismissive method of self-regulation is ultimately self-destructive because the emotions and meanings are "stuck," not moving through a natural course to resolution and acceptance. Ian's sexual acting out could have been his way of regulating himself. This, of course, is an anti-social means of re-regulation and in the long-run self-destructive, harmful to Ian himself.

Observations of School Personnel

Ian has an individual educational plan (IEP). As a fifth grader, he was reading at a third-grade level. He received remedial education for reading in a small classroom. Despite his difficulties with reading, the teacher said Ian is very smart. His math skills were excellent. In an incentive program that rewards children for excellent work, Ian kept the books for the tasks accomplished and the amounts of their awards. Ian excelled at gym, where he did gymnastics, plays volleyball, basketball, and baseball.

The school social worker said that Ian struggles with social skills in that he often holds himself back from interacting with other children, even when they try to engage him. Other children appear to like Ian. They include him in their activities and do not tease him. Recently, Ian talked with the school social worker about his father and seemed to want to spend talking time with her. According to the social worker, he appeared to be "missing his dad." The social worker considered Ian a "good kid" and "a treat." She said, "I love him to death."

Application of the NEATS

Neurobiology. Ian's reading difficulties could be neurobiological in origin. He has good brain functioning in terms of math and athletics.

Executive Function. Ian's intelligence is part of executive function, and the teachers believe he has high intelligence.

Attachment. Ian must be an appealing child for the school social worker to consider him a "treat" and to "love him to death." Also, he may have a secure attachment to the social worker because he talked to her about his father and appears to want to talk more about his father.

His hesitancy in interacting with other children could reflect issues with anxiety trust and therefore could be related to fearful, avoidant attachment. His inner working models of himself, others, and how the world works have been affected by his multiple traumas. His mother did not offer him a safe haven where he could work through his complex issue related to trauma and loss. Instead, she often modeled a dismissive attachment.

Self-regulation. Ian sometimes uses prosocial strategies of managing his distress, such as when he talks to others about his losses. These prosocial strategies are sporadic, and they are unlikely to be sufficient to result in good capacities for self-regulation. Ian does not show in-depth capacities for resilience. He is at risk to act in ways that reflect his own unmanaged traumas. Since he has experienced sexual traumas and many other dysregulating events that he has not dealt with adequately, he is at risk to act out sexually and may also be prone to depression. His mother had stated that she has been depressed since her husband died.

More Sexual Acting Out

When Ian was nine, he acted out with a younger boy while he on a sleepover with four other boys at a classmate's home. The boys slept in tents in the backyard. The parents allowed Ian to share a tent with the seven year-old son of friends who lived across town. Ian asked the boy to take his clothes off. The younger boy refused and ran into the house. Ian may have touched the boy sexually, although the details are not known.

The parents who hosted the sleepover were fond of Ian and were concerned about his history of multiple trauma and losses. They did not knew that he had aced out sexually with a younger child three years earlier. Marie did not believe Ian would act out and therefore allowed Ian to go on the sleepover.

Even after Ian acted out sexually a second time, Marie continued to be reluctant to get Ian into therapy. She said, "I don't see the value in rehashing this. It upsets Ian. It's hard for him to think about so he doesn't want to."

The school social worker said about this incident, "Ian had tons of shame about it. He couldn't even talk. They wouldn't even do sex specific treatment in that normal way with Ian because he's so far from being able to go there. He's got all that other grief and loss stuff that needs to be addressed therapeutically before they even get to that acting out." Ian cried often about his sexually acting out with the other boy.

The EXCEL service provider felt that it was a disservice that Ian had not received grief counseling, trauma therapy, and sex-specific therapy related to his multiple losses and traumas as well as his sexual acting. The provider believed that if she had been able to persuade Marie to get help years earlier, Ian would not have acted out sexually with the younger boy.

The younger boy showed signs of trauma. His parents reported that he developed anxiety reactions that he had not shown before. He became whiny and clingy. He screamed when his older brother accidentally intruded on him while he was in the bathroom. Within weeks after the abuse, the parents enrolled their son and themselves in a child sexual abuse treatment programs. They declined to press charges against Ian, who was 10 and old enough to be charged criminally.

They did, however, talk to Marie about their son's responses. Marie listened and expressed concern and sorrow. She told the EXCEL case manager that she was worried about Ian. He cried a lot and developed anxiety about leaving the home. He went to school reluctantly.

Application of the NEATS

Executive function. Once again, Ian did not consider the consequences for himself and the child he victimized. Had he received therapy for his grief, loss, and sexual issues, he would have learned that he could no longer be alone with younger children. Marie would have had professional help as well, and she would not have allowed Ian to go on an overnight.

Marie continues to show poor judgment in refusing to provide Ian with the professional services that he requires. Ian felt remorse after he acted out sexually, but he did not anticipate this remorse. Being unable to anticipate consequences shows a lack of executive skills.

Attachment. The pressure is mounting on Marie to do something to help her son. Marie loves her son and has all along done what she thought was right for him. Her inaction shows the depth of her dismissiveness.

Self-regulation. Ian showed incapacities to regulate his sexual behaviors. When in an unsupervised situation, Ian acted out sexually with another boy. Ian's sexual behaviors so upset the younger boy that the younger boy had difficulty regulating his own behavior.

Marie Allows a Full Schedule of Services

A few months after Ian acted out sexually a second time, Marie agreed to allow Ian to have a psychosexual evaluation. She said that he had been so unhappy she had to do something. When the psychologist asked Marie where Ian has learned about sexuality, Marie said "I haven't got a clue, maybe at school." Marie obviously had not talked to Ian about sex and sexuality.

Marie gave permission for Ian to have individual trauma therapy and sex-specific therapy. She engaged reluctantly at first and then enthusiastically in her son's treatment. After several months, she began her own individual therapy with a specialist in grief, loss, and trauma. Marie reported that working on herself was the hardest thing she had ever done. She said her therapist told her she has real courage.

Application of the NEATS

Executive function. Marie eventually realized that Ian needed help. She participated in her son's therapy. In this, she finally had good judgment. She also engaged in therapy for herself, which is another indicator of good executive function.

Marie had poor judgment in not providing her son with a good sex education, but good judgment in being honest to professionals about it. Children with sexual behavior issues are in special need of information about sexuality, sexual boundaries, sexual respect, and sexual abuse. That Marie refused grief, loss, and trauma counseling for her son was a serious disservice as well.

Attachment. Marie finally understood the seriousness of Ian's traumas and overcame her own beliefs about how Ian was supposed to handle stress. Her love and commitment led to good decisions about what is best for Ian. Ian was willing and even eager to engage in professional services, suggesting that he has capacities for hope and trust, qualities associated with secure attachments.

Trauma. Ian may have experienced a retriggering of trauma after he sexually acted out with the other boy. He expressed remorse for hurting the other boy and for causing him to be upset and anxious. Marie may have experienced trauma and relived previous traumas when she found out that Ian had once again acted out sexually. This second event and Ian's prolonged remorse must have shocked her into realizing that she had to get Ian some help and that she needed help himself.

Case Planning

The NEATS assessment has pinpointed issues related to neurobiology, executive function, attachment, self-regulation, and trauma in both son and mother. The issues identified through the assessment leads to comprehensive case planning. The following is a case plan based on the assessment.

Neurobiology. Ian would benefit from a neurological evaluation because of his learning problems. Although he has had an individual educational plan that includes special education for reading, the neurologist could recommend additional strategies to help Ian. A neurological exam may identify both strengths and risks that could be incorporated into case planning.

Teachers like Ian and spend considerable time with him to help him with his reading. This should continue.

Executive function. After many years of work with social services, Marie realized that Ian needed professional help and she did, too. Both are now fully engaged in therapy where they are dealing with the effects of their multiple traumas. There are many instances where Marie showed poor judgment, but those days look as if they are behind her.

Both Marie and Ian are learning a great deal about sexuality, boundaries, attachment, and self-regulation in the sex specific program and in their own therapy. Especially in the sex-specific program, psychoeducation is a major piece. Both Ian and Marie are learning a great deal about sexuality, sexual boundaries, and management of sexual behaviors after sexually acting out and after possibly being sexually abused.

Attachment. Mother and son appear to have a more secure attachment than in the past. While Marie had been dismissive of her own traumas and those of Ian, she has realized how deeply Ian had been affected. She came to understand that she needed help himself, after she participated in Ian's treatment. Marie never wavered in her commitment to Ian, but she had difficulties imagining that her son needed help, or that she did. Mother and son should continue to their therapy program and engage in the many activities that they enjoy together.

Trauma. Both mother and son experienced multiple traumas, and the therapy in which they are engaged hopefully will help them both to understand and manage the effects of their trauma. Ian and Marie may take years to work through the loss of Rick and the other traumas that they have experienced.

Self-regulation. Marie and Ian are learning to regulate their emotions through openly talking about them, understanding them, and expressing them in prosocial ways. They are learning to depend upon therapists to help them develop appropriate self-regulation skills. Ian will probably need therapy on and off throughout his life whenever he experiences a major life transition or a trauma. These negative life events could trigger episodes of dysregulation that could put him at risk to act out sexually or to shut down emotionally.

Until he started intensive services, Ian was on a pathway to become a juvenile and adult sex offender. With the kind of early intervention that he now has, there is reason to hope that he will not re-offend again.

Summary. This is a case of an 11 year-old boy named Ian with a history of multiple traumas. His mother Marie had refused specialized professional services until recently. Ian is in therapy for his trauma and is participating in sex-specific treatment program. His mother participates in her son's treatment, and she recently began individual therapy with a specialist in trauma and loss. There is reason to hope that Ian will not act out sexually again and will learn to regulate his emotions in prosocial ways. Therapy is promoting a secure attachment between mother and son and helping them to be less dismissive and avoidant. At present, Ian and his mother Marie are engaged in services that lead to hope that Ian will develop into an emotionally and psychological competent person.

A NEATS Analysis
of Childhood ADHD

Attention deficit hyperactivity disorder (ADHD) affects up to five percent of all children in the United States. The gender ratio is about five boys to every girl. Girls are more likely than boys to have attention issues without the hyperactivity or ADD. The origins of ADHD are not known definitively, but genetics may be factors for a large percentage of children with ADHD. Environmental factors such as maternal smoking and stress during pregnancy could also contribute to ADHD.

There are child and adult forms of ADHD. Typically, children with childhood ADHD contend with ADHD their entire lives, although the symptoms may modify over time. Characterized by difficulties with attention, control of activity levels, and impulse control, ADHD is a neurological condition that can be understood and responded to through an analysis that covers neurobiology, executive function, attachment, trauma, and self-regulation (NEATS). This chapter analyzes childhood ADHD using the five main concepts of the NEATS.

ADHD may occur with other childhood problematic issues and behaviors, such as learning disabilities, oppositional behaviors, bipolar disorders, complex trauma, and inadequate parenting. Sometimes children appear to have ADHD, but in fact they have experienced trauma that no one has helped them with, often complex traumas including abuse and neglect, witnessing violence, war, forced migration, parental death and abandonment, and multiple foster home placements. To respond adequately to children, they require accurate diagnoses of the roots of their behaviors. Children who have experienced trauma require care that differs from children with ADHD whose origins are genetic.

Although there are other types of ADHD, such as attention issues without hyperactivity and hyperactivity without attention issues, the type of ADHD discussed in the present discussion focuses on the combined type that includes issues with attention, activity, and impulse. The material is applicable to the other types with some adjustments.

Neurobiology

Two children are in a classroom where the teacher is explaining long division. They both hear the tweet of a bird and look out the window. On the branch of pine tree is a cardinal bird. One child turns back to the lesson, while the other flaps his arms like wings, tweets, and then shouts, "Look at that pretty bird."

What makes the differences in the behaviors of the two children? One possible explanation is neurobiology, or how the children's brains work.

Two ideas related to brain activity are excitation and inhibition. Excitation means that one part of the brain becomes stimulated and brain circuits fire. Inhibition means that another part of the brain puts on the brakes or provides a counterforce to the circuits that fire. If inhibition does not occur, brain circuits keep firing and individuals continue the behaviors that excitatory circuits influence.

This lack of counterbalance may operate in several different brain-based behaviors, such as ADHD, obsessive compulsive disorder, panic disorders, and depression.

In ADHD, children appear to have more than twice as much glutamate, a brain chemical called a neurotransmitter, than children without ADHD. Glutamate is a stimulant chemical that leads to excitation of neurons, which are the cells of the brain. Children with ADHD also have lower than normal levels of GABA which is a neurotransmitter that inhibits the stimulated neurons. GABA and glutamate counterbalance each other.

Applications

The child who looked at the cardinal and turned back to the lesson probably has normal levels of GABA and glutamate. He was interested in the bird and his glutamates may have kicked in, but GABA kicked back, and he realized that his task was to pay attention to the lesson. The child who tweeted, flapped his arms, and talked without anticipating consequences apparently did not experience a release of GABA. There apparently was no stopping his impulses to act out his interest in the bird. This child may have a lower level of GABA than other children and a higher level of glutamate.

Medication for ADHD

Stimulants, such as amphetamines, act as counterforces or inhibitors of the release of glutamates. Stimulants like these, therefore, reduce the behaviors associated with ADHD.

Most children with bipolar disorders also have symptoms of ADHD, but children with bipolar disorders have normal levels of glutamate.

These activities take place in the prefrontal cortex and the motor cortex where operations linked to attention, movement, impulse control, working memory, and language occur. These operations are called executive functions. The prefrontal cortex is the front of the brain and the motor cortex is on both sides of the brain.

Executive Function

Children with ADHD have issues with executive function. Executive function is a term that covers a broad range of capacities related to judgment, planning, anticipation of consequences, problem solving, and following rules and directions. Since the neurological roots of ADHD are in the prefrontal cortex, which is the seat of reasoning, it follows that children with ADHD have executive function issues.

It's important to note that when children do well when they have ADHD, their parents have excellent executive skills. Parents must be able to plan for and execute a family life that helps children with ADHD develop executive skills. Children with ADHD who grow up in families that follow schedules for meals, bedtime, homework, and recreation may internalize this structure and thus grain in executive skills.

In a structured family life, family activities take place on a predictable schedule. In addition, parents provide high warmth and affection, authoritative parenting that includes clear rules about what parents expect and what are acceptable behaviors and what are not, brief praise when children do something parents want them to do, and humane and brief consequences when children do not.

Consequences should never interfere with children's development, such as punishing children by limiting or eliminating playtime or forcing them to abandon a sport. Children with ADHD require the guidance of adults who have the executive skills to understand that all children, especially children with ADHD, can concentrate better and are more relaxed and happy if they have free time where they can play and exercise.

Parents of children with ADHD also require the executive skills to understand that they do better when they have the support and understanding of others and when they educate themselves about ADHD. There is a great deal of information available to parents. There also are parent support and education groups that they can attend.

Teachers, foster parents, professionals, and anyone else who comes in contact with children who have ADHD also will do well with these children if they have the executive skills to think through the consequences of their own behaviors and decisions for the children. School personnel, for example, often do not understand ADHD-related behaviors. Their responses to the children harm the children and may interfere with children's developing their potential, which is a loss to the children, their families, and to society.

The child who spoke without noticing whether others were speaking and who flapped his arms, and tweeted did not anticipate consequences or he dismissed any consequences that occurred to him. This is an example of poor executive skills. The child who thought about doing this thing but who refrained shows good executive skills. Both children could have ADHD, one of them could, or neither of them could. If they both have ADHD, then one child's case could be more severe than the other's or there are environment-based influences that might have affected each child's executive skills. An important environmental factor to consider is attachment.

Attachment

Two children born with a similar type of ADHD may have different behaviors as they mature. A reason for this could be differences in parental attachment styles. Parents with secure or resolved styles of attachment provide a safe haven where children can process everyday stresses and the extraordinary stresses that trauma can bring. To do well in life, children need the safety of secure attachments.

Other children and adults often do not know how to respond appropriately to children with ADHD. Without meaning to, their behaviors may hurt children with ADHD. These children need their parents and other adults to help them to understand the effects of their behaviors on others and what they can do to form mutual and happy relationships with other people.

This is not a simple task. Parents and other adults with secure attachment styles are positioned to be of great help to children with ADHD.

Parents who are preoccupied with their own issues or who dismiss the importance of their children's stressors will more often than not be unable to help their children with ADHD. They not only are psychologically unavailable to their children, but they also are insensitive to their children and unattuned to what children need to develop well. They will make things worse for their children. The children will come to believe that what they want and what they require to thrive is not important. They will learn that they are unimportant.

Some parents have so many issues of their own that they are disorganized in their behaviors, emotions, and thinking. Not only are they psychologically unavailable and insensitive to their children, but by their behaviors they are teaching children that disorganization is normal. Parental disorganization will make the behaviors associated with ADHD much more entrenched.

For children to do well when they have ADHD, parents must be psychological available and sensitively attuned. For this reason, parents must learn to manage issues they have that interfere with their parenting. If they do so, the will develop resolved attachment styles, and they will become psychologically available and attuned to their children. The issues that parents must deal with include unresolved histories of trauma, strife with partners, chemical dependency, untreated mental illness, and exposing children to family violence.

Childhood abuse and neglect can result when parents do not deal with their own issues. Unresolved parental issues can lead to trauma for children. Trauma is difficult for any child, but when they have ADHD, even one trauma becomes complex trauma.

If the two children who saw the cardinal perched on a pine had similar types of ADHD, then their attachment relationships could be a factor in why one showed good executive skills in that situation and the other did not.

Trauma

When children have ADHD, additional stresses can lead to even more pervasive issues with attention, activity, and impulse control. Trauma, in fact, can lead to children to behave as if they have ADHD, even if neurologically they were not born with it. Many children are medicated for ADHD when they have developmental stress disorder. If they received proper care for their trauma, their ADHD-like symptoms may disappear. Problems with attention, concentration, and hyperactivity are signs of trauma as well as ADHD.

When children are traumatized, memories of the trauma are encoded in the brain. Of particular importance is the hippocampus, which is where memories and contexts of memories are stored. The sights, sounds, smells, tastes, and physical sensations associated with the original trauma become encoded in the hippocampus. Often these memories and images are fragmented and are not stored as coherent stories.

When children encounter reminders of the trauma, brain circuits become activated and neurotransmitters are released. In ADHD, if there is too much glutamate and not enough GABA, then the children are at high risk to respond with increased symptoms of ADHD. Children without ADHD also are at high to respond in disorganized ways, but they also may be more able to cope with these responses that children with ADHD because they have normative levels of glutamate and GABA.

Dysregulation

Children with or without ADHD and who have been traumatized can deal with the effects of trauma to the point where they are able to cope with its effects, with on-going support from adults with good executive skills. These children may become disorganized temporarily, but they seek out adults they can trust and talk to them or at least seek comfort from them. They may talk later, after they are more regulated.

Children who do not have adults to go to and who are safe havens may learn to cope with reminders of the original traumas in antisocial, self-injurious, or inappropriate ways. They may throw chairs, get into fights, and threaten other children. They may cut themselves, overeat, or use drugs and alcohol. They may behave inappropriately, such as running around the classroom or getting on their hands and knees and barking like a dog.

Executive Skills of Adults

If the adults around the children do not have good executive skills and if they do not understand the nature of trauma and how children cope, they may respond punitively to children who behave in antisocial, self-injurious, or inappropriate ways. They may also dismiss the significance of children's desire for comfort with stress. If they do this, then they may discourage children from behaving pro-socially the next time they are stressed.

If the two children who saw the cardinal perched on a pine had similar types of ADHD, then their attachment relationships and their trauma histories are factors in why one showed good executive skills in that situation and the other did not. A child with a history of secure relationships and a history of trauma is more likely to have better executive skills than a child of insecure relationships and a history of trauma.

Self-Regulation

ADHD is characterized by issues with self regulation. Self-regulation stands for capacities to manage thoughts, emotions, and behaviors under everyday conditions. When children experience stress and trauma, varying degrees of dysregulation are expectable. By definition, children with ADHD have issues with self-regulation. Self-regulation is one of the executive skills, but because of its importance in work with children and their families, self-regulation is a separate category in a NEATS assessment.

Children learn to self-regulate through secure attachments and through living in families and being in schools and other settings that are safe, predictable, and where the adults model and reward capacities to regulate behaviors and structure environments so that children's capacities for self-regulation are enhanced.

Children's first experiences with self-regulation occurs in the earliest days of life, where, when they are stressed, parental care soothes them. Children internalize these experiences of stress and soothing and they become encoded in the brain. Eventually, children learn to self-soothe and also learn who soothes them and what activities soothe them.

All children thrive when they have structured, nurturing environments where rules are clear and desired behaviors are rewarded, but children with ADHD especially require such environments in order to maximize their potential. As discussed earlier, for children to develop effective self-regulation skills, they require long-term relationships with adults who have secure attachment styles, who are emotionally available and sensitively attuned, who deal constructively with their own issues, and who have good executive and self-regulation skills. When children have ADHD, adults who foster child development are knowledgeable about ADHD and know how to respond to children with ADHD.

Children with ADHD have trouble with self-regulation and require special considerations. Children with ADHD may be in dysregulated states not because they are re-experiencing trauma, but because of how their brains work. When they have experienced trauma, their dysregulated behaviors may increase in frequency and intensity.

A Case Analysis

A child with ADHD and unattended trauma may act in ways that uninformed adults believe is anti-social, defiant, and oppositional. For example, Jerry, age 8, was in special education because he could not regulate himself in a mainstream classroom. He had a diagnosis of

ADHD and oppositional disorder. No one recognized that he had experienced many traumas in his life including physical abuse and neglect and witnessing violence. There was no recognition that he had a disorganized style of attachment. They knew he often was reckless and showed poor judgment, but they did not interpret these behaviors as issues with executive function.

Jerry came to school one day very upset. He did not tell his teacher that his mother had pulled a knife on her partner that morning to get him to stop beating her. He did not feel safe enough to tell the teacher. Jerry pinched another child. The teacher told him not to do that. Jerry jumped out his chair, got down on all fours, and starting barking like a dog at the teacher.

The teacher called the vice principal who escorted Jerry to an intervention room where Jerry was alone for two hours. The detention room had concrete walls and a concrete bench on which to sit. The door was steel, with a window in it. About once an hour, the vice principal looked in on Jerry. He was curled in a corner, crying.

Jerry had dysregulated. Not only did his teacher not realize this, but the vice principal did not either. They did exactly the wrong thing for Jerry. Instead of trying to understand Jerry's inappropriate response to a reprimand, they behaved in punitive ways. Jerry dysregulated even more. He learned nothing about how to re-regulate in prosocial ways.

Jerry was part of a family that was abusive and neglectful and a school system that misunderstood the stress and trauma he experienced daily. School personnel missed an opportunity to help Jerry learn how to regulate his behaviors more appropriately and to provide him soothing and comfort for his trauma.

However children dysregulate—no matter how strange the behaviors seems—the first principle is to make sure the children are safe. If the children's behaviors threaten others, then their safety also is paramount. Children who are dysregulating should not be left in a room by themselves. At least one adult should be close by, watching for the right time to re-direct children's distress. The adults can gently call the children's name in the hope that the children will respond and begin to re-regulate.

Once the children appear to have re-regulated, they can then help the children to process their distress. If appropriate, adults can touch the children and comfort them physically. Parents and other care providers can do this but professionals such a teachers and social workers may have to follow professional guidelines.

In encouraging children's self-expression, adults can start with "How are you doing?" and "Are you okay?" and "Something set you off. What happened?"

Many children, especially younger ones, will be eager to state what had been going on. Children may process the events through words perhaps, or drawings, or through acting out important episodes with toys. Eventually the adult can help the children to problem-solve about how to respond to the situations that led to dysregulation.

If the children learn to trust their teachers and school administrators, these adults can serve as safe havens for the children. Other adults may not be able to undo the effects of years of parental abuse and neglect, but they can make contributions to children's executive skills, including their capacities for self-regulation,

Many factors play into children's issues with self-regulation. Any additional stressors they experience will increase their tendencies to dysregulate.

Discussion

Core issues for children with ADHD are neurobiological, executive function, and self-regulation. Secure attachments help optimize executive skills and capacities for self-regulation. When children with ADHD experience trauma, secure attachments are key to dealing with and managing the effects of trauma. The five dimensions of the NEATS, therefore, are important in understanding ADHD. Effective socialization of children with ADHD requires an implicit or explicit understanding of the NEATS and of ADHD itself.

References

Anderson, Peter (2002). Assessment and development of executive function (EF) during childhood. *Child Neuropsychology, 8(2)*, 71-82

Courvoisie, Helen, Stephen R. Hooper, Camille Fine, Lester Kwock, & Mauricio Castillo. (2004). Neurometabolic functioning and neuropsychological correlates in children With ADHD-H: Preliminary findings. *Journal of Neuropsychiatry and Clinical Neurosciences, 15,* 63-69.

Davies, Douglas (2004). *Child Development: A practitioner's guide (2nd ed.).* New York: Guilford.

Gilgun, Jane F. (2010). *Shame, blame, and child sexual abuse: From harsh realities to hope.* Amazon Kindle, scribd.com/professorjane, and other on-line book sellers.

Gilgun, Jane F. (2010). *The NEATS: A child & family assessment.* Amazon Kindle, scribd.com/professorjane, and other on-line book sellers.

Lieberman, Alicia F. (2004). Traumatic stress and quality of attachment: Reality and internalization in disorders of infant mental health. *Infant Mental Health Journal, 25(4),* 336-351.

Mash, Eric J., & David A. Wolf (2007). *Abnormal child psychology* (4th ed.). Belmont, CA: Wadsworth.

Moore, Constance M, Joseph Biederman, Janet Wozniak, Eric Mick, Megan Aleardi, Megan Wardrop, Meghan Dougherty, Terri Harpold, Paul Hammerness, Edin Randall, Perry F. Renshaw (2006). Differences in brain chemistry in children and adolescents with attention deficit hyperactivity disorder with and without comorbid bipolar disorder: A proton magnetic resonance spectroscopy study. *American Journal of Psychiatry, 163,* 316–318.

Van der Kolk, Bessel A. (2005). Developmental Trauma Disorder: A new, rational diagnosis for children with complex trauma histories. *Psychiatric Annals 35(5), 390-398.*

Wozniak J., Biederman J., & Richards J.A. (2001). Diagnostic and therapeutic dilemmas in the management of pediatric-onset bipolar disorder. *Journal of Clinical Psychiatry, 62,*10–15.

10

A NEATS Assessment
of Children with Serious Conduct Issues

This chapter shows that the NEATS can help identify and organize important information about serious conduct issues. Many children can learn to manage their conduct issues with an accurate assessment and parental willingness to deal with their own issues while at the same time taking good care of themselves.

There is a great deal of research, theory, and clinical experience about children with problematic and even dangerous conduct issues. When practitioners apply this information to particular cases, they find they have a lot of information. The NEATS can help organize this information. The NEATS leads to accurate understandings. Accurate understandings, in turn, lead to effective case planning, education, policy, treatment, and prevention efforts. Above all, accurate understandings provide parents, teachers, and other adults with guidelines on how to respond and not respond to children with antisocial behaviors.

Because human development takes place in contexts and most of these contexts involve interactions with others, an application of the NEATS requires assessments not only of the person who is of interest, but also other people and events that may have influenced development over time.

I defined the terms of the NEATS here and have discussed them in more detail in the first several chapters of this book.

A NEATS Assessment

Neurobiology

Conduct issues may have neurological roots that are present at birth or they may arise later through experiences with other people. Neurobiology refers to brain structures and functions that result from the interaction of genes with environmental conditions. Sometimes children inherit predispositions for conduct issues. Whether or not these predispositions get expressed depends upon how powerful the genetic influences are, whether there are co-occurring limits to brain development, and how parents manage their own stresses.

Temperament appears to be neurobiological in origin and children who develop conduct disorders often have difficult or "slow to warm up" temperaments from birth. Difficult or slow to warm up temperaments can be managed well in families whose "NEATS" factors are predominantly positive and the families do all they can to get the information, emotional support, and medical and emotional care that helps them to maintain sensitive responsiveness. Such parenting may help children manage a predisposition to behaviors that are antisocial, behaviors that are grouped under the category "conduct issues."

If, however, parents do not have capacities to self-regulate and to maintain sensitive responsiveness, there is likelihood of additive effects, or risk pile up. In other words, in families who have unmanaged vulnerabilities within the categories of the NEATS, a child with vulnerabilities for conduct issues is at higher risk to develop them. These families cannot provide the consistency, sensitivity, role modeling, and discipline that children require for optimal development. Children with neurobiological vulnerabilities require all of the above and, in addition, the family requires accurate information, emotional support, and, in most cases, professional consultation.

Executive Function

Executive functions (EF) are compromised when children have conduct issues. Children with conduct issues do not think about or do not care about the effects of their behaviors on others, or they do not understand the hurt that they inflict, even as some may enjoy hurting people on the surface. They also do not think through the consequences of their antisocial behaviors for themselves, either, or they tell themselves they can get away with it. Consequences include social isolation. Other children may dislike and avoid them, and they become lonely, frustrated and even more vulnerable to EF issues, to their detriment and to the detriment of persons with whom they come in contact.

Indicators of good parental EF when children have serious conduct issues include using professional help, obtaining as much information as they can find, seeking emotional support and even respite for themselves, and taking good care of themselves while at the same time maintaining their commitment to their children. In short, parents with good EF do all they can to maintain sensitive responsiveness to their children.

When children with conduct issues have parents who have poor EF, this adds to children's vulnerabilities to develop chronic issues with antisocial conduct. If their parents have antisocial conduct issues themselves, this also increases children's risk. If parents' behaviors lead to child trauma, this affects the likelihood that children, with or without neurobiological vulnerability to develop conduct issues, will develop them. Parents whose behavior leads to child trauma have deficits in their EF. When parents have deficits in their EF, they are are poor role models for their children. A core idea of EF is understanding consequences of your own behaviors.

Sometimes parents have excellent EF and have no apparent neurological issues or manage whatever neurological issues they do have. Still, their children could serious issues with their conduct. In other words, children may have conduct issues even when parents have done all they can to be sensitive and responsive.

Children who have conduct issues and their parents require professional consultation. One of the first steps to be followed is to evaluate child and family for the possible roots of the issues.

Attachment

Attachments that are secure can moderate many of the genetic/neurobiological vulnerabilities to conduct issues, such as infants with difficult or slow to warm up temperaments. Through parent behaviors associated with secure attachments, infants typically develop secure styles of attachments themselves and the good EF and SR associated with secure attachments. In other words, through sensitive, responsive care, children with vulnerabilities for difficult temperaments may develop capacities for self-soothing and for prosocial self-regulation. They also develop prosocial expectations about themselves, others, and how the world works secure attachments. They develop positive self concepts, such as believing they are loveable, worthy of love, and loving.

Parents require support and information in order to maintain these secure relationships with infants whose temperaments are difficult. If parents have unresolved traumas or difficulties with EF and self-regulation, then they may be unable to handle the difficulties of having an infant who is difficult or slow to warm up. Infants with these temperaments have trouble engaging in reciprocal interactions consistently.

Reciprocity and mutual regulation are rewards that parents experience in their care of children. Reciprocity and mutual regulation involve positive feedback loops, such as when parents smile and children smile back, or when children turn away when they want to stop interacting with parents and parents let the children be. Children who are unresponsive and even actively reject parental attempts to soothe them are unsatisfactory to parent. This in turn may create negative feedback loops that could leave to parental avoidance of interactions with their infants.

Expectations of how interactions will go become part of the processes of parent-child interactions. These expectations affect how parents and children interact with each other. Expectations become parts of both parents' and children's inner working models of their relationship. Children typically generalize these early IWM and apply them to interactions with people other than their primarily attachment figures.

Parents who have secure or resolved styles of attachment have learned to manage any neurological issues they may have and also have learned to manage effects of any trauma they may have experienced. They also have good EF and self-regulation skills. They have capacities for trust and good intuition about who is trustworthy. Thus, they make good judgments about who are trustworthy professionals who can help them with their children, and they have the good judgment to seek support and information.

Parents who have insecure styles of attachment, such as dismissive, preoccupied, and disorganized, not only may be inconsistently sensitively responsive to their children, but they will have compromised EF and difficulties with self-regulation. Some of these parents may also cause trauma in their children through abuse and neglect, which includes creating unsafe family environments. Their care may be so inadequate that it is pathogenic; that is, it is severely detrimental to children.

Children hit the jackpot in terms of risks when they have neurological issues that put them at risk for conduct issues and their parents have deficits in their styles of attachment. If parents also have unmanaged neurological issues and behaviors lead to children trauma, then, without a great deal of compensatory experience, children with vulnerability for conduct issues will develop them. Even children without vulnerability to trauma may develop them under severe adverse conditions.

Pete's case study in chapter 7 is an example of a child who may have been born with some predispostion to neurological issues and whose mother and father had poor executive skills and disorganized and dismissive styles of attachment. Pete developed such serious conduct issues that he was placed in a psychiatric hospital twice by the time he was eight.

Pete's father divorced his wife, got treatment for cocaine addiction, and was active in Narcotics Anonymous for two years when the court awarded him full custody of Pete, who was then eight and still in the hospital. At first the father was dismissive of the seriousness of Pete's conduct issues, until he saw them first-hand. Then he did whatever he could to help his son. Pete's behaviors gradually stabilized as his father provided the structure, predictability, and emotional stability that Pete—and any child—requires to develop secure relationships (attachments) and good EF.

Trauma

Trauma is inevitable throughout the life course, from infancy to old age. Children may experience birth trauma, which can create early anxieties and may affect brain development. The mothers may experience post-partum depression, which is more common than many people realize. Post-partum depression may compromise mothers' capacities to be sensitively responsive. Fathers and other caregivers may be distracted or unavailable to compensate for the emotional unavailability of mothers with depression. The "baby blues," not as debilitating as depression, may also affect mothers' capacities for sensitive responsiveness.

Without compensatory care from others, children may find everyday stressors to be overwhelming because parents are not available to soothe them and to help them to re-regulate. Such infants may develop early difficulties with self-regulation. They may also develop inner working models that indicate that the world is not safe and care providers are unreliable and untrustworthy. Such IWMs place children at risk to develop problems with SR and EF.

When children experience trauma, they require the safety of secure relationships to work out issues related to trauma. They also require education and training on how to manage issues with self-regulation that are inevitable effects of trauma. Many professionals believe that children require proficiency in self-regulation before children are guided to deal directly with the effects of trauma. Meditation, yoga, thought switching, positive self-talk, talking to trusted others, and vigorous exercise are just some of the ways that children can learn to regulate their emotions, thoughts, and behaviors.

Parents with secure styles of attachment are central to helping children deal with their own traumas. If parents have unmanaged trauma, they must obtain professional help so that they can provide the safety, empathy, and guidance that children require to learn to manage the effects of trauma. When parents have dismissive, preoccupied, or disorganized styles of attachment, by definition they have issues with their own traumas. They may be unable to provide what children need to overcome effects of trauma.

Children with unmanaged trauma have difficulties with SR and EF. They are at risk to manage the effects of their trauma inappropriately and self-destructively. If they have been exposed to models of violence and gain any pleasure or enhanced sense of well-being by acting out in antisocial ways, they are at special risk to use antisocial means to self-regulate.

Ian, 11, whose case is discussed in detail in chapter 8, experienced multiple traumas before the age of six. The traumas included being sexually abused, witnessing domestic abuse, seeing another child beaten to death, and the death of his father, all by the time he was six. His mother thought it was better just to put these traumas behind him. She did not get him professional help until he was ten years old and had developed sexual acting out behaviors.

Self-Regulation

Children with conduct issues are unable to regulate their emotions, behaviors, and thoughts in prosocial ways. Their parents have been unable to help them to learn prosocial ways of self-regulation and may even have been the prime role models for children's antisocial behaviors. This is not always the case, for sure, because "good enough parents" sometimes have children with conduct issues. The roots of conduct issues can sometimes be outside of parental control. Many different experiences and neurobiologically-based vulnerabilities may be the foundation of conduct issues, despite parents' best efforts and despite the efforts of other adults, such as other family members, teachers, and experts in child development.

In many families where children's conduct is of concern, it is worthwhile to look at any issues parents may have with self-regulation. Children often learn how to self-regulate through how parents behave. Issues with parental self-regulation may have what appear to be minor consequences for parents, but when children take on these same strategies they may have much bigger consequences. Children do not have the executive skills to anticipate consequences that parents do. Therefore rather innocuous parental deficits in SR could have major consequences for children when they emulate their parents.

At the dinner table one evening, Jim, a father of four, rapped his eight year-old son Michael on the head with a fork so hard the fork bounced and made a "clunk" sound. Jim was angry because his son had spilled peas. His wife Margreta said nothing. Five year-old Maria witnessed the incident. Two days later, Maria rapped a classmate on the head with a ruler because the classmate had stolen her pencil. Maria got in big trouble.

Maria's mother later explained that it is wrong to hit other children. "When someone does something you do not like," Margreta said, "tell an adult." Maria said, "Daddy hit Michael." Margreta asked, "How do you think Michael felt?" Maria said, "It hurt." Margreta said, "Do you want to hurt other people?" Maria said, "No." Margreta said, "Don't forget that. Hitting other people hurts them. Use words. Do not hit other people." Maria never again hit another child or anyone else.

Maria had the executive skills and the self-regulation to understand what her mother told her and to control her behaviors the next time someone did something she did not like. Overall, she had received "good enough" parenting. Her stepfather, however, modeled hurtful behaviors. A simple "Whoops" when Michael spilled the peas would have sufficed. The mother could have spoken to her husband about his unkind act in the children's presence. This would have modeled how to express disapproval of unkind behaviors. Jim then could have modeled how to apologize and take responsibility for unkind acts.

The NEATS and Social Service Systems

The NEATS can also be helpful in assessing quality of service provision. For example, what are the executive function issues involved in multiple child placements in foster care? What guides the decision-making of professionals who leave children in biological families whose parents have unmanaged issues with mental illness and chemical dependency and who inflict trauma on their children with regularity?

Jake, 12, lives with his mother who is an alcoholic who is drunk every day. Jake's mother has beaten him several times. Jake calls the police for help. The police typically tell the mother to knock it off, but one time the police took Jake to the hospital to protect him from his mother's rage and to get him medical care. He told the police and child protective social workers that he never wanted to live with his mother again. The next day, when the mother visited him in the hospital, she said she did not want him to come home. Jake went into foster care. Within five days, child protection had placed Jake back with his mother. They put no services in place and closed the case. His mother beat him the next week. Jake did not call the police, but left the house and wandered the streets until he thought his mother had passed out. A few weeks later, he grabbed a woman's purse after he told her he had a gun in his pocket. He used the money to buy marijuana.

Such examples of poor executive function on the part of social service professionals are all too common. What are they thinking? What do they think is going to happen with Jake when they keep him in such terrible circumstances? Service providers often have unexamined assumptions about their own roles in clients' lives, how they use their power, and whether they engage in dialogue, work by fiat, or are indifferent and permissive.

Jake would benefit from a NEATS assessment and careful case planning. So far in his life, he has not received the services he has required. Without intensive services, he is at risk to continue his antisocial behaviors. Jake is showing poor executive skills. Professionals who can help him would have to have excellent executive skills, policies that support good case planning, and resources to offer him.

Another question that arises from NEATS assessments of service provision includes the following. Are services providers sensitive and responsive to child and family issues? The ideal is authoritative practice, which means that professionals are aware of their professional power and use it judiciously. They also interact with clients and other professionals with high sensitivity, empathy, willingness to listen and negotiate, and to engage in partnerships. They respect client autonomy and dignity, but they also know that in some cases they are agents of social control, whose job involves protecting children—and adults—from harm and promoting their well-being. They therefore have to set limits on parents' abusive and neglectful behaviors. They know and act upon the principle that parents' authority ends where children's well-being and rights are violated.

The services that Jake and his mother received were not like this. Child protection did not set limits on Jake's mother, but instead placed Jack back with his mother. The did not act on the principle that parents' authority ends when children's well-being and rights are violated. In Jake's case and in the case of many other children, in the long run the rights of society for safety are at risk when children develop conduct issues.

Summary of the NEATS Assessment For Conduct Issues

The following summarizes information relevant to a NEATS assessment for conduct issues.

Neurobiology

- neurobiological influences on children's conduct issues may or may not be present;

- if they are present, they increase vulnerability for the development of conduct problems;

- if they are not present, environmental conditions can influence brain development and children become "soft-wired" for conduct issues; this wiring, however, can be modified because experience continually remodels the brain's wiring;

- environmental conditions that lead to infant and child stress can interact with genetic vulnerabilities that in turn lead to problematic conduct issues; as stated, children with little apparent neurobiological predispositions to conduct issues may develop them under conditions of stress whose effects are not repaired through consistently sensitive and responsive parenting;

- parents of children with neurobiological risks for conduct issues may have neurobiological risks themselves; and

- best practice is for service providers to assess parents, children, and other immediate family members, such as parents' siblings, and children's grandparents for conduct issues and other neurological conditions.

Attachment

- secure attachments can help moderate vulnerabilities for conduct issues that are linked to neurobiology;

- parents may require extra resources to maintain secure relationships with children who have neurologically-based vulnerabilities for conduct disorders;

- when parents have insecure attachment styles that include dismissive, preoccupied, and disorganized types, this adds to the risks that neurobiological vulnerabilities pose;

- when children experience trauma, they require the safety of secure relationships to adapt to, cope with, or overcome the effects of trauma, in other words, to become resilient;

- pathogenic care practically guarantees that children will have conduct issues, independent of the presence or absence of neurological vulnerabilities.

Executive Function

- by definition, problems with executive function (EF) is a characteristic of conduct issues;

- parents with good executive functions are likely to have secure styles of attachment;

- children with neurological vulnerabilities and who have parents with good executive skills may learn to manage issues related to their potential for antisocial conduct;

- the converse is also a viable hypothesis; namely, children with neurological vulnerabilities for conduct issues have an additional risk when their parents have poor executive skills; such parents also are highly likely to have insecure attachments.

Note:

This chapter is taken from the book, *Children with Serious Conduct Issues* by Jane F. Gilgun, Ph.D., LICSW, that is available from on-line booksellers as a download or paperback.

References

Anderson, Peter (2002). Assessment and development of executive function (EF) during childhood. *Child Neuropsychology, 8(2)*, 71-82.

Arendt, Robert E. et al (2004). Child prenatally exposed to cocaine: Developmental outcomes and environmental risks at seven years of age. *Journal of Developmental and Behavioral Pediatrics, 25(2), 83-90.*

Cairns, Kate (2002). *Attachment, trauma, and resilience: Therapeutic caring for children.* London, UK: British Association for Adoption and Fostering.

Davies, Douglas (2004). *Child Development: A practitioner's guide (2nd ed.).* New York: Guilford.

Gilgun, Jane F. (2009). *The NEATS: A Child & Family Assessment.* Available at Amazon Kindle, scribd.com/professorjane, and stores.lulu.com/jgilgun.

Gilgun, Jane F. (2006). Children and adolescents with problematic sexual behaviors: Lessons from research on resilience. In Robert Longo & Dave Prescott (Eds.), *Current perspectives on working with sexually aggressive youth and youth with sexual behavior problems* (pp. 383-394). Holyoke, MA: Neari Press.

Greene, Ross W., & J. Stuart Ablon (2006). *Treating explosive kids: The collaborative problem-solving approach.* New York: Guilford.

Gilgun, Jane F. (2005). Evidence-based practice, descriptive research, and the resilience-schema-gender-brain (RSGB) assessment. *British Journal of Social Work. 35 (6)*, 843-862.

Lederman, Cindy S, Joy D. Osofsky, & Lynne Katz (2007). When the bough breaks the cradle will fall: Promoting the health and well-being of infants and toddlers in juvenile court. *Infant Mental Health Journal, 28(4)*, 440-448.

Hinshaw-Fusilier, Sarah, Neil W. Boris, & Charles H. Neanah (1999). Reactive attachment disorder in maltreated twins. *Infant Mental Health Journal, 20(1)*, 42-59.

Lieberman, Alicia F. (2007). Ghosts and angels: Intergenerational patterns in the transmission and treatment of the traumatic sequelae of domestic violence. *Infant Mental Health Journal, 28(3)*, 422-439.

Lieberman, Alicia F. (2004). Traumatic stress and quality of attachment: Reality and internalization in disorders of infant mental health. *Infant Mental Health Journal, 25(4)*, 336-351.

Mash, Eric J., & David A. Wolfe (2007). *Abnormal child psychology* (4th ed.). Belmont, CA: Wadsworth.

Perry, Bruce (2006). Applying principles of neurodevelopment to clinical work with maltreated and traumatized children. In Nancy Boyd Webb (Ed.), Traumatized youth in child welfare (pp. 27-52(. New York: Guilford. Website at www.childtrauma.org and click on the link CTA's Neurosequential Model of Therapeutics.

Shaw, Daniel S., Arin Connell, Thomas J. Dishion, Melvin N. Wilson, & Frances Gardner (2009). Improvements in maternal depression as a mediator of intervention effects on early childhood problem behavior. *Development and Psychopathology, 21*, 417–439

Shonkoff, Jack P., & Deborah A. Phillips (Eds.). (2000). *From neurons to neighborhoods: The science of early childhood development.* Washington, D.C.: National Academy Press.

Sokol, Robert J., Virginia Delaney-Black, & Beth Nordstrom (2003). Fetal Alcohol Spectrum Disorder. *JAMA, 290(22)*, 2996-2999.

Summers, Susan Janko, Kristin Funk, Liz Twombly, Misti Waddell, & Jane Squires (2007). The explication of a mentor model, video-taping, and reflective consultation in support of infant mental health. *Infant Mental Health Journal, 28(2)* 216-236.

Teicher, Martin H. (2002). Scars that won't heal: The neurobiology of child abuse: Maltreatment at an early age can have enduring negative effects on a child's brain. *Scientific American, 286(3)*, 68-76.

Thapar, Anita et al (2003). Maternal smoking during pregnancy and attention deficit hyperactivity disorder symptoms in offspring. *American Journal of Psychiatry, 160(11)*, 1985-1989.

van der Kolk, Bessel A. (2005). Developmental Trauma Disorder: A new, rational diagnosis for children with complex trauma histories. *Psychiatric Annals 35(5), 390-398.*

van der Kolk, Bessel A. (2006). Clinical implications of neuroscience research in PTSD. *Annals of the New York Academy of Sciences, XXXX,* 1-17.

Weatherson, Deborah J., Julie Ribaudo, & Sandra Glovak (2002). Becoming whole: Combining infant mental health and occupational therapy on behalf of a toddler with sensory integration difficulties and his family. *Infants and Young Children, 15(1),* 19-28.

11

A NEATS Analysis of Children
with Autism Spectrum Disorders (ASD)

This chapter describes a NEATS analysis of autism spectrum disorders (ASD). It also shows that with an excellent assessment in many cases early intervention can change developmental pathways so that some children with the potential for ASD can join the social world and succeed in school.

Autism spectrum disorders (ASD) are pervasive developmental disorders characterized by three general classes of behaviors: difficulties in relating to other people in reciprocal, empathic ways, difficulties communicating through language, and restricted and repetitive behaviors and interests. Within these classes of behaviors, there is a large range of variation.

More than two-thirds of children with ASD have co-occurring mental retardation, and the other third have normal or high IQs. Most also have co-occurring language delays, and some children with ASD never develop language skills. Many children have repetitive mannerisms, such as handflapping, spinning, smelling objects, pacing, starting at rotating fans, and lining up objects. It is as if they are in the own exclusive and excluding worlds. Some have echolia, which means they repeat words that others have just said.

Some children with ASD have sensory issues, meaning that they are especially sensitive to certain sights, sounds, smells, text, textures, and touch. Some develop difficulties with self-regulation that can be in the form of physical aggression toward others such as hitting, biting, and kicking. Self-injurious behaviors, such as head-banging, arm biting, and scratching.

Others may have trouble regulating their emotions and may scream, cry, and throw themselves around when something happens that they do not like.

Some children with ASD may have special talents in art, music, and other activities, while still having mental retardation and language difficulties.

This chapter describes autism spectrum disorders (ASD) and shows that in many cases early intervention can change developmental pathways so that some children with the potential for ASD can join the social world and succeed in school.

Conditions Along the Spectrum

The pervasive developmental disorders along the autism spectrum are autism, Asperger's disorder, Rett's disorder, childhood disintegrative disorder, and pervasive developmental disorder not otherwise specified. Each of these conditions begins in infancy or early childhood. Children with Asperger's have impairments in social interactions, a restricted range of interests, and normal to high IQs, with little or no delay in language skills. They often give the appearance of "little professors," not only because of their body posture and manner of speech, but also because of their detailed interest and knowledge of one topical area, such as the weather, dinosaurs, or football.

In their intense focus on issues of interest to them, they appear oblivious to others, which can have negative effects on siblings and other children who may feel discounted and left out. In such situations, a helpful response is for parents or other adults to redirect children with ASD and engage with the other children. Having separate time with children and psychoeducation of children can counterbalance the effects of obliviousness.

Children with disintegrative developmental disorders reach developmental milestones within normal limits, but between the ages of two and ten begin to lose skills previously acquired, such as language, social interactional skills, and motor skills. Children with Rett's disorder develop within normal limits for the first five months of life and then not only lose previously acquired skills but develop severe impairments in language and physical coordination. They engage in stereotyped behaviors such as hand wringing. Between the ages of five and 48 months, their head growth decelerates. Mental retardation, often profound, are characteristic of these disorders.

Differential Diagnosis

ASD is differentiated from selective mutism, a condition in which children have language skills in some situations and do not have deficits in the two other conditions associated with ASD. Children with only one of the three classes of behaviors associated with ASD receive other diagnoses, such as expressive language disorders and mixed expressive disorders.

If children with mental retardation have the other two classes of behaviors associated with ASD, they are classified as ASD. When children have symptoms of childhood-onset schizophrenia (COS), such as delusions and hallucinations, in addition to the classes of behavior associated with ASD, they are give the diagnosis of COS and ASD. Decades ago, children with ASD were diagnosed with COS, as ASD was not well-known and not well-defined enough for psychiatrists, psychologists, and social workers to make that diagnosis. When children have symptoms of attention deficit hyperactive disorder (ADHD) and ASD, they are not given the diagnosis of ADHD.

This brief overview provides only a glimpse of the variability of the conditions categorized as pervasive developmental disorders or autism spectrum disorders.

A NEATS Analysis

A NEATS analysis may help organize the complex information that is now available for assessment, case planning, intervention, and evaluation. Furthermore, the NEATS alerts practitioners about what is important to assess and thus provides the foundation for effective interventions. NEATS is an acronym that stands for neurobiology, executive function, attachment, trauma, and self-regulation.

The NEATS is ecological, meaning that practitioners gather information about the five components not only on the children, but on parents, siblings, and other family members in the extended family. Also, the NEATS guides practitioners to consider developmental and historical influences on children, such as parents', grandparents', and other family members' histories of trauma, issues with self-regulation, neurological conditions, attachment histories, and executive functions.

Attachment as Foundational

The NEATS is based upon the assumption that attachment is foundational to human development. Children born with neurological issues, for example, will have a good chance of optimal development if their care providers have capacities for secure attachments and resources to promote development, such as access to expert educational opportunities.

With neurological issues such as ASD, however, there are ceiling effects, where, because of limitations imposed by neurobiology, no further development is possible even in the best of circumstances. In many cases, we do not know enough nor are resources available to foster children's development to the point where they reach ceiling effects, but in some cases ceiling effects appear to be at issue.

Guidelines for Using the NEATS

The components of the NEATS are linked. For example, if the presenting issue is self-regulation, then professionals investigate possible neurological underpinnings, how executive functions operate, whether individuals have experienced trauma, and how the quality of attachments affects the other dimension of the NEATS. If the presenting issue is neurobiological, professionals collect information about the neurobiological issues themselves and how neurobiology has affected the other four dimensions.

In addition, service providers assess for how the other dimensions, trauma and attachment in particular, affect neurobiology. Relevant family members are part of the assessment, including their developmental histories, consistent with the ecological, developmental aspects of the NEATS.

Assessment for trauma is another example of how to use the NEATS. When children have experienced trauma, professionals assess for quality of child-care provider attachments and issues with self-regulation and executive function. They do social histories to assess whether parents own trauma histories may interfere or be helpful in work with children who have experienced trauma. Trauma may also affect brain functioning.

Children who have been traumatized will have issues with self-regulation, executive function, and attachment. In addition, their brain circuitry can be affected.

Recovery from trauma becomes problematic when histories of unattended trauma are discovered in their parents and other family members, as well as histories of issues related to the other four areas of the NEATS. As with other condition, children have the best hope of recovery from trauma within the safety of secure relationships.

The prognosis is more guarded if their care providers are unable to provide the safety of secure relationships. Parents with insecure attachment styles also are unlikely to seek professional help and other resources that can help their traumatized children recover. Trauma is no advantage to children with ASD and can further complicate an already complicated array of behaviors and issues.

Summary

The NEATS guides practitioners to assess for five areas of human development that researchers have identified as fundamental to human development. The NEATS is ecological and developmental.

When children have ASD, parents with insecure and even disorganized styles of attachment and experiences of unattended trauma complicate the already complicated developmental processes, and their prognosis more guarded. Children with ASD and other childhood condition reach optimal development within the contexts of secure relationships where they have the resources required to foster their development.

Definitions

The following are brief definitions of the five components of the NEATS. They serve as a review and summary of the earlier chapters in this book.

Neurobiology is a branch of biology concerned with the anatomy and physiology of the nervous system, especially the brain, under various conditions of health, stress, and pathology. Neurobiological systems are the foundation for how we think, feel, and behave, while simultaneously, how we think, feel, and behave shapes the workings of our brains. Who we are as human beings is inseparable from how our brains work. Brain development results from an interaction of genetics and environmental events that occur prenatally, at birth, and postnatally.

Notions of ceiling effects and brain plasticity are important in the neurobiology of ASD. Ceiling effects mean that even under optimal conditions, there may be limits on degrees of neurological development and therefore limits on the degree of development within the three domains that ASD affects. The plasticity of the brain, on the other hand, represents the potential for human brains to reshape itself over the life course in response to environmental events.

Two main processes characterize brain plasticity: pruning and increases in neural connections (and, sometimes the generation of new neurons, but this is beyond the scope of the present book). Infants are born with many more brain cells, or neurons, than they will eventually use. Through a kind of "pruning" process that the "use it or lose it" principle influences, the human brain sheds those neurons that go unactivated. Human experience shapes which neurons are put to use and which are not. Also in response to experience, neurons form new connections throughout life that supports the retention of various capacities, including motor skills, language acquisition, and reasoning.

Executive function (EF) is a term that covers a broad range of capacities related to judgment, problem-solving, organization of self, anticipation of consequences, and following of rules and directions. Regulation of emotion and behaviors is part of executive function as well, but in the NEATS assessment, self-regulation is a separate category because of its significance to human behavior and functioning.

Attachment is defined as behaviors that maintain contact with individuals who serve as a secure base from which to explore and to which to return under times of stress, as well as to serve as a source of nurturance and love. In addition, for children, attachment figures provide guidance and discipline, including limit setting, boundary maintenance, authoritative parenting, and contingent responsiveness and reciprocity. Secure attachments foster optimal brain development in children, which promotes good executive skills.

Trauma is defined as an event that is life-threatening or psychologically devastating to the point where persons' capacities to cope are overwhelmed. Trauma may change brain structures related to memory and emotion, as well as brain circuitry. Following trauma, individuals relive the traumatic event, fragmented memories arise unexpectedly, cognitive, emotional, and behavioral dysregulation occurs, and there is avoidance of reminders of the event.

Self-regulation (SR) is defined as capacities to manage and make sense of one's own thoughts, emotions, and behaviors in times of stress and in the course of everyday life. Some view self-regulation as one of the executive functions. Capacities for self regulation are both genetic in origin as well as the results of experience. Subjectively, children experience dysregulation as a loss of control, of unmanageability of thoughts, emotions, and behaviors. Heart rate and breathing may become accelerated.

When dysregulated, individuals throughout the life course may become fearful, anxious, withdrawn, depressed, hyperactive, lethargic, and experience emotional outbursts, bed wetting, sleep disturbances, and oppositional behaviors. Some individuals are euphoric while in dysregulated states.

To learn to reregulate in prosocial ways, children require the safety of secure relationships, guidance as to how to handle episodes of dysregulation in the future, and immediate, brief praise for any signs of capacities for prosocial self-regulation, such as telling a parent, "I'm getting angry. Can I have a hug?"

Summary and Discussion

A NEATS analysis not only organizes information about children's functioning within these five categories, but it also organizes information about the NEATS-related issues of parents, siblings, grandparents, and other relevant members of the extended family. A NEATS analysis of the behaviors and resources that service providers offer also can be helpful in treatment planning, expectations for outcome, and evaluation. In addition, social policy can be analyzed in terms of the executive functions of policy makers.

The NEATS, therefore, is ecological in scope and takes into account a complex array of influences on child and family function. Finally, a NEATS analysis is developmental, guiding practitioners to gather information about child and family history and any other historical influences of children and their families.

In the next sections, I discuss ASD using the categories of the NEATS.

Neurobiology

ASD are classified as neurodevelopmental conditions. This means that ASD have a biological basis and that brain structures and functions are foundational to their origins. Factors identified in the development of ASD include genetics, environmental events, and their interactions. The most hopeful outcome of the discovery of possible genetic-environmental interactions is that in some cases the course may be modified through structured, planned interventions. The earlier the identification the better. So far, the earliest reliable identifications are at age 12 months. There is accumulating evidence of earlier markers, which is good news because it makes very early intervention feasible.

Younger siblings of children with ASD are at higher risk than other children to develop an ASD, although only a small percentage have the condition. As a result, siblings typically receive screenings during infancy and early toddlerhood. Parental involvement in conjunction with the guidance of expert practitioners are characteristic of situations where interventions influence the developmental course for the better, when and if the genetic loading is not so high as to preclude modifications of developmental pathways.

Genes, Environments, and Their Possible Interactions

Combinations of genetic susceptibility and environmental events are leading hypotheses about the origins of ASD. At present, there are many "candidate" genes that researchers think may be linked to ASD, but further research is required. Furthermore, different combinations of genes may have variable interactions that in turn learn to variable outcomes in children. Researchers hypothesize that some ASD appear to be on a developmental timeline that starts with genetic susceptibility, or genes that are expressed under a range of environmental events.

Environmental events may occur during gestation, such as when the fetus is exposed to chemical toxins, medications that the mother takes during pregnancy, or to viruses. At the time of birth, birth accidents and trauma may be a factor, including restricted oxygen intake. Post-natal changes in children with ASD have been observed. For example, head size of some infants who develop ASD are within normal limits at birth, but grow larger during first year of life and then over the next years return to be within norms. This is thought to be associated with less "pruning" of neurons during this period as well as the development of large and underdeveloped neurons in parts of the brain and thick growth of neurons in other parts of the brain.

The origins of these developments are unknown, but they are likely to have a strong genetic component. Allergies and inabilities to metabolize various substances found in food are thought to have effects. Some children may have special sensitivities to caseins and glutens, and some benefit restricting items containing them from children's diets. Environmental toxins may play a role prenatally and postnatally in the development of ASD. There is little evidence that mercury compounds in childhood immunizations are factors.

Mutations of particular genes during gestation may play a part in some forms of ASD. Whether these mutations are related to environmental events is not known.

Family studies also support the hypotheses of genetic and/or gene-environment interactions. Concordance among identical twins is as high as 91% and among fraternal twins is 6-8%, higher than within the general population, which is about .5 to .25%. Some people appear to carry genes for ASD but they are not expressed, more so in women than in men.

The origins of disintegrative developmental disorders are not known, but they are unlikely to be related to genetic-environmental interactions, but from a neurological pathology linked to genetics. Rett's disorder appears to linked to mutations in a specific gene. Male fetuses with this mutation die. Researchers and clinicians question whether this developmental disorder and Rett's disorder are related to ASD, despite similarity of symptoms. Both of these conditions are rare.

Genetic Loading and Overpowering Environments

As applicable as the hypothesis about genetic susceptibility and environmental events may be to some forms of ASD, there are likely to be situations where the genetic loading is so powerful that no matter how favorable environmental events are, infants are born with ASD because of their genetic makeup alone. It is also possible in some cases that the environmental risks are so powerful that infants develop ASD without genetic susceptibility. For example, Harlow's monkeys that were raised with wire mothers developed behaviors that replicated the behaviors of children with ASD.

Involvement of Many Parts of the Brain

Imaging studies, autopsies, and electro-encephalograms show that ASD can affect many different parts of the brain including the cerebellum, the frontal lobes, mirror neurons, hippocampus, and amygdala, among others. For example, the bigger the decrease in the neural circuits in the amygdala, which is the site of emotion meaning and memory, the more severe are children's social impairment, including capacities for reciprocal, social interactions.

Mirror neurons may play a role in ASD. Mirror neurons are inter-related brain structures and circuits that become activated when individuals see other persons performing actions, experiencing sensations, or expressing emotions or when the individuals themselves are doing so. In persons with ASD, the mirror neurons do not become activated when they view others in these circumstances. These neurons, however, become activated children with ASD themselves are performing actions or having similar experiences.

Researchers believe that mirror neurons are associated with learning by observation and in the development of empathy and in perceiving the intentions of others. Some research suggests that the degree of mirror neuron activity is related to capacities for social interaction; the less activity, the more diminished are the capacities. When there are higher degrees of activities, there are more capacities.

Researchers have uncovered conflicting evidence about the involvement of any one brain structure. They have, therefore, hypothesized that ASD results from interrelationships among a number of brain structures. As in other brain-based conditions, there are hypotheses, supported by some evidence, related to inhibitory and excitatory synaptical connections and brain circuits. Excitation and inhibition are basic notions of brain chemistry. When one part of the brain becomes stimulated, another part of the brain puts on the brakes. If this does not happen, brain circuits keep firing and individuals continue the behaviors that excitatory circuits influence.

Neurochemistry therefore is involved in at least some ASD, such as lower levels of dopamine which is associated with reward responses and care provider-child attachments. Dopamine also is important in amygdala development. Glutamates, which are excitatory neurotransmitters, may play a role in ASD, as well. The neurotransmitter GABA inhibits the neurons that glutamate stimulates. In ASD, there is an imbalance between the interplay of GABA and glutamates.

Autopsy studies show inflammation of neurons in some individuals with ASD. The origins of the inflammations are not known but could be related to the biochemistry of the brain and gene-based sensitivity to various chemicals and viruses that might not affect others without the susceptibility.

Infant Temperament

Infants with predispositions for ASD can be passive or fussy, including being highly reactive, difficult to soothe, or both. Not all children with temperament issues develop ASD, a very important point. Even parents with secure attachment styles themselves, lots of social support, and a great deal of knowledge may be challenged to offer consistent, sensitive, and response care to children who do not cue that they want, who are non-responsive to cues for mutually pleasure interactions, or who are fussy and hard to soothe.

When parents are unable to provide consistent, responsive, and sensitive care then children's neurobiologically-based difficult behaviors may become even more difficult. This is yet another example of the interactions between neurobiology and environmental events.

Physicians sometimes subscribe medications for children with ASD. Medication may help with some of the behavioral issues associated with ASD and with possible co-occurring conditions such as attention-deficit hyperactivity disorder, but there is little evidence that medication affects the core issues of ASD.

Summary

ASD are neurodevelopmental conditions that have a wide range of variations. While researchers and practitioners have greatly advanced knowledge particularly in the last decade, Identification of origins is important for prevention and intervention.

Executive Function (EF)

Children with ASD have serious issues with judgment, planning, anticipation of consequences, and problem-solving, almost by definition because EF is so closely linked to neurobiology. They may not, for example, anticipate the consequences of their lack of reciprocity in social situations because they may be unaware of the rewards built into social interactions. Children who act aggressively toward others or who injure themselves do not anticipate the full range of consequences of these behaviors for themselves and others.

The same may be true of other behaviors that set them apart from other children. Many children with ASD, therefore, may have limited EF, although some and possibly many may know something is not quite right for them, but they may not know what it is.

Intelligence is often considered one of the executive skills. As mentioned, more than two-thirds of children have some form of mental retardation. In addition, as many as 25% of individuals with ASD have "islets of abilities" or special abilities such as in drawing, music, and mathematics.

Children with ASD require close adult supervision if they lack the executive skills to keep themselves safe and pose risks to others. Adults with ASD and deficits in executive skills cannot live independently. They may live in group homes or with aging parents or with other family members.

Attachment

The percentage of children with ASD and who have secure attachments to care providers may be similar to children without ASD. The children with ASD have much more subtle attachment behaviors. For example, mutual regulation and attunement are characteristics of secure attachments. Children with ASD may experience these kinds of interactions. It may be difficult for others to perceive signs of such mutuality, but some parents report that on some level they feel the mutuality with their children even if outward signs are not present.

Yet, and this seems contradictory, symptoms of ASD complicate formation of attachments, which, as mentioned, is based upon neurobiological capacities such as reward systems that dopamine represents. If there are low levels of dopamine, then infants do not experience much reward through reciprocal interactions and parents' sensitive, responsive care.

Parents of children with ASD require considerable support to provide the sensitive, responsive care that all children require. Parents who are unable to provide this care complicate already complicated developmental pathways.

Children with ASD who have responsive parents are likely to find their parents serve as secure bases and provide them with opportunities to develop inner working models of self, others, and how the world works that maximize their opportunities for optimal development. Without secure relationships, children with ASD are likely to develop inner working models that lead them to anticipate confusion, rejection, and a sense of being different.

Capacities for attachment broaden to other children and to other people in general as children grow older. Children with ASD have, by definition, issues with social interaction. As they grow older, many have few if any friends and engage in solitary activities. Adults with Asperger's and others with high functioning autism often marry, have children, and in general live out their lives in ways similar to adults without ASD.

It sometimes is said that children with ASD are more interested in objects than in people. Whether and how this operates in individual lives is subject to testing to see if and how such a statement fits and what can be done to stimulate pleasure in social interactions.

Trauma

Children with ASD may have more trouble dealing with traumatic events than children without ASD. This is a possibility if they have few capacities for dealing with their emotions and if they do not show the effects of trauma but remain passive and apparently unmoved. It is possible that children with some forms of ASD do not have the brain circuitry within which trauma is encoded. This, of course, is highly speculative but as a working hypothesis for practitioners, this may be helpful in providing sensitive, responsive interventions.

What is also likely is that trauma affects capacities for self-regulation, attachment, and executive functions, as well as subsequent neurological developments including the encoding of schemas or inner working models, as difficult to discern as some effects may be.

Unattended trauma that children with ASD experience is likely to complicate children's ASD symptoms and make additional contributions to difficulties with EF and self-regulation. Within the safety of secure relationships, children with ASD who are experienced trauma are likely to do adjust better than children who do not have the safety of secure relationships.

Until there is evidence to the contrary, parents and professionals serve children well when they assume that trauma affects children with ASD in similar ways to children without ASD. As in all childhood situations, adults tailor their responses to fit children's capacities.

Self-Regulation

Children with ASD often have major issues with self-regulation that contribute to the perceptions of others that they are odd. Passivity and reactivity that are characteristic of ASD are regulatory issues whose foundations appear to be neurological. Thus children may have highly disruptive and even dangerous behaviors including throwing objects and other behaviors already discussed such as self-injurious and destructive actions.

Over time, with experience within the safety of secure relationships, children may learn to regulate their passivity and reactivity, but they may become life-long issues. For example, when Jay was a pre-schooler, he had major tantrums when his parents asked him to stop an activity, such as lining up his toy cars, and come to dinner. As he grew older, such reactivity diminished considerably, but he continued to experience agitation in making transitions from one activity to another.

Children with ASD may hide behind furniture, not respond when called, and generally ignore people around them. Such passivity in relationship to other people represents incapacities to regulate their behaviors to stay in tune with others.

Sensory issues, which may co-occur with ASD appear to complicate capacities for self-regulation and contribute to high reactivity. Children with ASD who hear loud noises may scream, cry, and throw themselves on the floor, rather than having a simple startle response and return to whatever they were doing.

The repetitive movements that children with ASD often perform may represent incapacities to regulate their movements within generally accepted social norms. They may also be efforts at self-soothing and self-stimulation.

Preoccupations are regulatory issues. For example, Lily, five, was preoccupied with lint. Wherever she was, she crawled on the floor to inspect rugs for lint. She collected little piles and then proudly presented them as gifts to her parents and other care providers. These gifts suggest capacities for attachment and hopes and expectations for a thank you. Yet, her parents and other care providers could not help regulate those behaviors and therefore walk into a room and start playing with toys, instead of looking for lint.

Discussion

ASD represent complex sets of behaviors that can challenge parents, siblings, teachers, and classmates. Siblings of children with ASD require special attention in order to offset any possible negative effects of the ASD-related behaviors. Parents have to be especially aware of focusing on the children with ASD while overlooking the attachment-based needs of their other children.

Psychoeducation can increase the patience and understanding of persons who come in contact with children with ASD. Children require sensitive responsiveness, consistency, and guidance about what are acceptable and unacceptable behaviors. The more understanding other people have of ASD, the more likely they are able to respond in helpful ways.

Psychoeducation includes grappling with one's own emotional responses and examining one's own executive functions and self-regulation capacities. Information can facilitate these capacities, but in some cases parents and service providers find that they require professional help to deal with the deeper personal issues that children with ASD bring out.

Competent parents and professionals do whatever it takes to make things better for children, including learning to forgive themselves when they make errors of judgment. Self-forgiveness, however, is the beginning of making repairs for damage done. Other steps include seeking consultation and support not to repeat the error and education about how to promote the well-being of children under their care.

Early Identification of ASD

Symptoms of ASD may appear early in infancy, but researchers have found that reliable indicators appear after age six months and are most reliably detected by ages 12 to 18 months. Many of the identification approaches are behavioral and interactional. There is increasing evidence that neurophysiological evaluations, such as using EEG and some brain imaging, may detect ASD even earlier.

Home videos of children celebrating their first birthdays were among the earliest pieces information that showed indicators of ASD in infancy. Children who later developed ASD were rather solemn and disengaged from the festivities, while home videos of children who subsequently developed along typical lines showed the babies laughing, interacting happily with others, vocalizing in other ways, clapping their hands, and showing enjoyment as they ate the cake.

Parents often are concerned about their very young children, but sometimes medical professions wait for one or more years before they make the diagnosis. Many researchers and clinicians are engaged in efforts to educate medical and social service professionals about the early signs of ASD so that interventions can begin at the earliest possible time.

One of the earliest behavioral indicators is the failure of infants to respond to their names. Hearing loss, off course, has to be ruled out. The Autism Observation Scale for Infants (AOSI), designed for the use of trained observers, pulled together many of the early behavioral signs of ASD. The AOSI measures behaviors associated with development of ASD and is used with infants between the ages of six to 18 months. These behaviors include

- Visual tracking, or the capacity to follow a moving object across a midline;
- Disengagement of attention, of the capacity of shift attention from one attractive object to another;
- Eye contact;
- Response to a smile with a smile;
- Imitation of the behaviors of others, such sticking out the tongue when the examiner does;
- Atypical gaits;
- Repetitive hand or finger motions; and
- Social babbling.

Early Intervention

The good news about the influence of environmental events on subsequent development is the emerging evidence that when ASD is identified in infancy and toddlerhood, then developmentally appropriate interventions may influence neurological development. In this way, some of the most devastating effects of genetic predisposition are offset. Children can then increase their capacities for social interaction, expressive and receptive language, and engage in activities that other children without ASD enjoy. The effects of early interventions can be so favorable that many children

Children with predispositions to ASD and who do not have mental retardation and language disorders appear to respond well to early intervention, but even then there is no guarantee that every child will. Mental retardation and language disorders complicate the design of early intervention, and there is reason to provide every child with ASD early intervention no matter what their symptoms may be.

The figure below shows the hypothesized interactions between genetic susceptibility, negative environmental events, and the development of ASD.

Figure 4: Interactions of Genes & Environment in the Development of ASD

The figure below shows interventions can modify the development of ASD.

Figure 5: Interactions of Genes & Environment in the Development of ASD

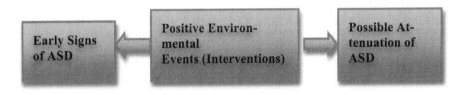

Early Intervention and Neurological Development

The goals of early intervention are to influence neurological development, so that the neurological pathways for ASD do not become established. Studies of enrichment programs on baby animals provide some of the bases for early interventions for human babies. Researchers have documented many favorable changes in brain structures and circuits with associated changes in behaviors as a result of enrichment programs.

Several studies with rats and primates show increased weight and densities of the neocortex, which are areas of the brain responsible for higher mental processes, as well as in the hippocampus. There also are positive effects on neurotransmitter receptors. Associated outcomes included improvements in memory, reduction of fearful responses and increased exploration of novel situations, and adaptability to new situations. These studies give great hope for enrichment experiences for children with ASA because the favorable outcomes are in domains in which children with ASD have difficulties.

Studies have also shown that animal enrichment can offset the effects of early trauma. Animals with genetic brain conditions show increased branching of the dendrites (the branches of neurons that form circuits), increases in balanced neurotransmitter activities, and increases in exploratory behavior. Enrichment programs, however, do not influence the core features of genetic brain conditions, such as the proteins that may be involved. This lack of influence of enrichment programs demonstrates the principle of ceiling effects.

Finally, animal studies demonstrate the possibility of critical periods; that is, developmental stages in which the effects of interventions are optimized.

Parental Involvement

Early intervention programs for children with ASD have a significant parental component consistent with the principle of the centrality of attachment in human development. These programs are intensive and long term. They start when children are between the ages of one to four and require 20 to 25 hours per week for a minimum of two years and sometimes longer.

The programs target the behaviors that researchers, practitioners, and parents have identified as problematic, such as activities to encourage imitation, social play with others, language development, self-regulation, and adaptations to new situations. Applied behavioral analysis involves immediate positive recognition of desirable behaviors and redirection and containment of undesirable behaviors.

The staff who work with parents are highly trained and competent, and there are frequent reviews of children's progress. This may involve observations of children with their parents and with other children at the program and at home. Videotaping of parent-child and child-child interactions is an important teaching tool. Professionals review the tapes with parents. This leads to discussions about specific behaviors in specific contexts and the development of strategies to increase desire behaviors and decrease others.

Documented Good Outcomes

While there are many promising programs, few have completed rigorous evaluations. The UCLA Young Autism Project has had such an evaluation. The children entered the program at the average age of 32 months. The children in the experimental group participated in special education classes and had ten hours per week of one-on-one instruction. The children in controls groups received special education only.

At age seven, almost half of the children in the experimental group had normal or high IQs and had completed mainstream first-grade class without extra supports. For this group, their IQs increased from an average of 70 to 107. At age 13, the results were similar. Children in control groups did not have these achievements. For example, only one of the 40 children in these groups completed mainstream first grade without supports.

There are many promising programs built solidly on research that will undergo intensive evaluation within the next few years. It is clear that intensive early interventions that target the issues that are prevalent in ASD work for large numbers of children. Improvement depends not only upon the severity of the ASD but also upon parental capacities to participate and the competence of professionals.

The principles of infant mental health (IMH) can be helpful to early intervention programs. These principles include working with both parents and children, helping parents deal with their own issues that may interfere with their sensitive responsiveness, educating parents about their children's issues, asking questions such as, "what do you think is going on for your child right now?," and providing running commentaries on children's activities that educate parents about child development.

Infant mental health practitioners also fill many of the roles that social workers and other service providers typically fill, such as making referrals, coordinating services, helping parent to secure resources such as food and medical care, and advocacy. The service requirements of families where children have ASD can be extensive.

In some locales, such intervention programs and other services are unavailable. Internet parent support groups, consultations through email, and consultations with professionals through webcam transmissions can be of help in these situations. Parents, for example, can videotape their interactions with their children, send the files to practitioners who review them, and then consult through webcam. Internet parent support groups can provide both information and social support that parents of children with ASD typically require.

Discussion

ASDs are pervasive developmental disorders that are neurobiological in origin and that affect major areas of human development and interaction. Early intensive interventions that involve a team composed of parents and professionals show promise in offsetting the development of conditions associated with ASD. Such programs have good results with many children, but not all children benefit for a variety of reasons. These reasons are related to the severity of the condition, parental capacities, and professional competence. Access to these programs is a significant issue that contemporary technology can partially offset.

Much is known about ASD, its origins, course, and effective interventions, but much more needs to be known. Practitioners who work with children and their families require on-going training and supervision to gain and maintain competence. More early intervention programs are needed, more parent support and education resources are required, as are on-going process and outcome evaluations of these programs.

References

Autism Speaks. www.autismspeaks.org An especially informative website

Bryson, Susan E., Lonnie Zwaigenbaum, Catherine McDermott, Vicki Rombaugh, & Jessica Brian (2008). The Autism Observation Scale for Infants: Scale development and reliability data. *Journal of Autism and Developmental Disorders, 38,* 731-738.

Cairns, Kate (2002). *Attachment, trauma, and resilience: Therapeutic caring for children.* London, UK: British Association for Adoption and Fostering.

Coffey, Kenneth M., & S. John Obringer (2004). A case study on autism: School accommodations and inclusive settings. *Education, 124 (4),* 632-640.

Davies, Douglas (2004). *Child Development: A practitioner's guide (2nd ed.).* New York: Guilford.

Dawson, Geraldine (2008). Early behavioral intervention, brain plasticity, and autism spectrum disorder. *Development and psychopathology, 20,* 775-803.

Mash, Eric J., & David A. Wolfe (2007). *Abnormal child psychology* (4th ed.). Belmont, CA: Wadsworth.

Rutter, Michael (2006). Autism: Its recognition, early diagnosis, and service implications. *Journal of Developmental and Behavioral Pediatrics, 27 (Suppl.),* S54-S58.

Weatherson, Deborah J., Julie Ribaudo, & Sandra Glovak (2002). Becoming whole: Combining infant mental health and occupational therapy on behalf of a toddler with sensory integration difficulties and his family. *Infants and Young Children, 15(1),* 19

12

A NEATS Analysis
of Child Physical Abuse

Child physical abuse threatens children's psychological and physical health and is a symptom of callousness and inhumanity in adults who perpetrate it. Despite the consequences of physical abuse, most parents physically abuse their children at least once. A large percentage of parents physically abuse their children as a routine part of their childrearing.

A NEATS analysis shows the importance of using alternatives to physical abuse and even alternatives to physical discipline. The NEATS is a child and family assessment that directs practitioners to five areas of human development that research has established as fundamental. These five areas are neurobiology, executive function, attachment, trauma, and self-regulation. NEATS is an acronym that stands for the first five letters of these terms. Each of these five

Definition of Child Physical Abuse

Child physical abuse involves strikes against children's bodies that damage children's spirit and that may also cause bruises, bleeding, broken bones, disability, and death. For the purposes of this discussion, *spiritual injury, emotional injury,* and *psychological injury* are rough synonyms. These injuries mean that children believe they are bad, deserve to be treated badly, and can do nothing to change their status as bad. In addition, children believe themselves to be powerless to influence the behaviors of others. They therefore are at the mercy of others, forced to put up with behaviors that they may not like and find hurtful. Each instance of physical abuse adds depth to these beliefs. Over time, these beliefs become deeply embedded and difficult to change. If children experience other forms of abuse and neglect, the damage is compounded.

Acts of abuse range from a single slap, punch, or kick to multiple strikes that lead to cuts, bruises, burns, other physical injuries, physical disability, and death. The strikes against children's bodies may be with hands, fists, feet, or other parts of other persons' bodies; with object such as sticks, knives, guns, belts, whips, and switches; with moving objects such as vehicles; with hot or burning objects such as cigarettes, irons, and hot water; and with strikes of children's bodies against walls, floors, or between pieces of wood. Research documents that children with disabilities, such as cerebral palsy, deafness, and blindness, are at higher risk for physical abuse—and other kinds of abuse and neglect--than children who do not have disabilities.

No matter what behaviors children have exhibited, there is no justification for physical abuse. There is reason to believe that optimal child development requires the complete absence of physical abuse. Furthermore, physical punishment itself is problematic for children's emotional and psychological well being. If parents do slap or spank occasionally, parents must be clear to children why they are being punished this way. Parents must also provide guidance and positive recognition for behaviors that parents want children to perform.

Consequences for Children

Besides risks for physical injury and death, child physical abuse hurts children psychologically, emotionally, and spiritually. Children can and do recover from the effects of child physical abuse. In terms of recovery from physical injury, children require excellent medical care. Skull fractures and other breaks in bones, as well as damage to soft tissue through blows, and to skin through burns can be life-threatening and have life-long negative consequences. Some children have long-term brain injuries that affect capacities for learning and for physical mobility. Damage to soft tissue can result in loss or impairment of hearing, kidney function, and liver function, among other damages. Fortunately, with optimal care, both medical and within the context of loving families, children can recover from physical abuse, even the effects of severe abuse. Some children, however, have life-long disabilities. Some die.

Children who have experienced physical abuse and do well when they receive the medical care they may require and also have people they can go to who comfort them, help them to deal with the repercussions of being physically abused, and protect them from further physical abuse. Many children who have experienced physical abuse develop empathy for others who experience hardships. They go on to live lives characterized by competence in relationships with others and in their activities, such as schoolwork and eventually paid work.

Children who are not fortunate enough to experience this kind of care have a range of responses that often do not serve them or others well. These responses can be placed into three rough and imperfect categories:

- avoidance of conflict and compliant behaviors;
- ambivalence and aggressive behaviors; and
- preoccupations and withdrawn behaviors.

Sometimes a single category fits a particular child, as when a child is fairly consistently compliant and conflict avoidant. These children often have issues with anxiety, fearful because they anticipate the next instance of physical abuse as coming at anytime. Some children show all three types of responses, depending upon the circumstances.

Children harmed by physical abuse have areas of strength where they do well under safe circumstances. They engage in a range of activities and may be able to form satisfying relationships with others. In situations where they feel safe, they also may be able to stand up to the aggression of peers. Some children become "model children," which may work well in circumstances when the expectations advance their well being such as learning in school. Being model children may work against them when the demands are unreasonable. These children may be unable to resist others who invite them into activities that go against their interests. They may, for instance, participate in antisocial acts such as vandalism with other children, even when they prefer not to. They also may give in to the sexual advances of others when they prefer to refrain.

Other children may show the effects of child physical abuse by being physically abusive and aggressive themselves. Often they behave this ways in situations where they feel unsafe. For example, some children do quite well in school but have issues in neighborhoods and home. Some are aggressive in every situation. They behave in aggressive ways because they think that is how they are supposed to act in situations where they feel threatened. They may misperceive situations to be threatening when others intend no threat. They may also find that doing to others what others have done to them makes them feel better. They may enjoy intimidating others. Physical aggression soothes their spiritual hurt. In situations where they feel safe, they may get along quite well. They may even be charming, engaging, and considerate.

Still other children may behave in ways that work against them, such as being withdrawn and fearful of interacting with others. As with aggressive responses to threat, children who are avoidant and withdraw may be outgoing in situations where they feel safe, but not in situations where they perceive threats. Because they know first-hand what physical abuse is, they may think about physically abusing others in order to comfort themselves and to feel as if they have some power to influence others. They may not act out these thoughts, but they are at risk to harm themselves.

These children are often lonely and afraid. Other children tend to avoid them. Even adults may find them unappealing.

Sensitive Responsiveness After Physical Punishment

Sometime parents are not physically abusive but use physical punishment to force child compliance and assert their authority. While I prefer that parents do not use physical punishment, some believe in it, especially because children usually stop the unwanted behaviors. If children express hurt after spankings and other physical punishments, parents must listen quietly and not be dismissive or overanxious about what children say. Once the children have shared their experiences of physical punishment, parents can express empathy for the hurt, explain the reasons they used physical punishment, state their preferences to use reasoning and rewards, and explain how children can behave in appropriate ways and that lead to parental approval.

If parents have struck their children out of anger, or because they were angry at someone else or another situation, parents can tell the children they are sorry. They can also say they still don't want the children to behave as they did, but that they were wrong to strike out in anger. In the future, they will make efforts to use words of guidance and disapproval, but not physical punishment.

Physical punishment works in the short-term. Children comply, usually. In the long-term, however, children can be hurt and angry, which not only affects relationships with parents, but with others, and also can contribute to beliefs about being bad and unworthy. Children may also vow to get back at parents or be aggressive toward others. To offset these effects, parents must build bridges when their children after a bout of physical punishment, without washing away their disapproval of inappropriate behaviors.

The following is a helpful general principle: Parents can listen to children and be sensitively responsive to children's hurt and even apologize for inflicting hurt, and they can still require children to behavior appropriately. Appropriate behaviors are actions and beliefs that respect other people and that are honest expressions of emotions and desires.

Alternative Parental Behaviors

Parents and other adults can teach children to behave in socially appropriate ways without resorting to physical punishment or physical abuse by

- Being emotionally available to children;
- Being interested in children's activities;
- Spending time doing mutually enjoyable activities with children;
- Helping children name their emotions;
- Guide children to express their emotions and wants in appropriate ways;
- Be clear about expectations for children's behaviors;
- Give clear explanations for why certain behaviors are not permissible;
- Give clear directions about what children can do to express their emotions and get what they want without infringing on the rights of others;
- Give brief penalties such as time out when children express emotions inappropriately or attempt to get what they want by disrespecting others after parents have explained appropriate ways of conducting themselves; and
- Give rewards for compliance with parental expectations, such as "Thank you," or "Good job."

In general, the alternatives to child physical abuse and physical punishment include sensitive responsiveness, clear expectations, and structure in terms of family and child activities. The above list defines these terms. Physical punishment risks psychological damage to children and to parent-child relationships if parents do not attempt to build bridges afterward.

On the other hand, child physical abuse is wrong. It harms children. It creates mistrust and fear in children. It harms parent-child relationships and sibling relationships. Physical abuse may cause physical injuries and long-term disabilities Children transfer their mistrust of parents to other persons. They may have difficulties forming satisfying relationships with peers and adults outside the family. They may experience problems in school and later on problems in work because of mistrust of others and lack of guidance about how to develop relationships of trust.

Children who experience physical abuse are at risk to physically abuse other children and to grow into adults who physically abuse others, including their own children and their spouses. They may also be at risk to harm themselves and/or cut themselves off from other people. A NEATS assessment provides direction on how to offset risks associated with physical abuse.

If children's unwanted behaviors persist after consistently using the above approaches, parents would do well to consult with a pediatrician for guidance. Children may have neurological issues that predispose them to challenging behaviors, or they may have experienced traumas that parents do not know about. Parents might require education about these issues, and they may benefit from parents support groups as well. Further details about treatment plans appear later in this chapter and in a paper listed in references.

A NEATS Assessment

The following discussion applies the NEATS to child physical abuse. The purpose of this discussion is show how the NEATS helps to identify key issues, helps to organize information that results from assessments, and helps to guide helpful responses to child physical abuse. In addition, there are massive amounts of information now available about child physical abuse. This information is disorganized and hard to remember. The components of the NEATS are easy to remember and thus can help parents and service providers identify and organize this information and to evaluate how and whether this information helps them to understand particular situations.

The NEATS is a handy way for parents to identify and organize information about themselves and their children. Service providers who know the components of the NEATS have a handy way to identify and organize information about the families and individuals with whom they work and to guide their work with families. A book-length discussion of the NEATS (Gilgun, 2010) is available on the Internet.

Neurobiology

Neurobiology is a branch of biology concerned with the anatomy and physiology of the nervous system, especially the brain, under various conditions of health, stress, and pathology. Neurobiological systems are the foundation for how we think, feel, and behave, while simultaneously, how we think, feel, and behave shapes the workings of our brains. Who we are as human beings is inseparable from how our brains work. This is a direct quote from the book *The NEATS: A Child & Family Assessment* (Gilgun, 2010).

Brain development results from the interactions of persons with their environments. The experiences children have from birth, and even while developing in the uterus, affect how their brains develop. Genes contribute to brain development and so do experiences. From the genesis of eggs and sperm onward, environments and genes are in interaction, mutually shaping each other. These interactions are often called nature-nature interactions, where nature stands for the contributions of the genes and nurture is the contributions of the environment to human development.

Optimal brain development takes place under optimal environmental conditions. During gestation, these conditions include good prenatal care, healthy maternal nutrition, maternal sense of safety and security within families and communities, and absence of diseases, infections, and chemicals that can affect fetuses adversely.

When pregnant women experience physical abuse, children's neurological development is affected. The stress of physical abuse releases hormones in women. These hormones can cross the placenta and affect fetal brain development. Stressed pregnant women may also not eat well and may use chemicals and/or medications that can affect fetal brain development. They can become preoccupied to the point where they miss doctor's appointments.

At birth, there appears to be three general types of infant temperament: easy, difficult, and slow to warm up. "Easy" babies probably have few neurological challenges and are easy to engage in interactions. "Difficult" babies may be resist engaging with parents and others and may even push away from physical contact and refuse to interact. They have various degrees of neurological issues that may or may not place limits on their development. Some may be difficult to comfort. They cry for hours every day. "Slow to warm up (SWU)" babies appear to be wired so that it takes them time to respond to attempts of others to engage them.

Compared to the other two temperaments, "easy" babies statistically are the least likely to experience parental physical abuse as compared to the other two types. On an individual level, however, parents who have belief systems and stress levels that place them at risk to physically abuse children probably will abuse even infants who are "easy."

The lack of interaction and resistance to interaction that difficult and SWU babies show can trigger frustration and anger in susceptible parents. This places these children are high risk for parental physical abuse. Sometimes long bouts of crying can lead to parental shaking, slapping, spanking, and even throwing of babies. This is physical abuse.

If the physical abuse results in head injuries, children may have brain damage. Even without physical injury to child brains, the psychological effects of physical abuse shape brain development. The experiences of fear, mistrust, and discomfort associated with physical abuse become encoded in children's brain circuits. Repeated instances of physical abuse strengthen the connections of the neural pathways that encode responses to abuse. Terror, fear of annihilation, and other catastrophic fears can become encoded in the brain.

These dynamics can play themselves out over the years that parents raise their children. The more routine physical abuse is, the more strongly encoded in the brain are the effects of physical abuse. The encoding happens as brain cells, called neurons, develop connections with other neurons. Connections are made through the development of dendrites which branch out at the ends of neurons. Neurotransmitters, which are chemicals that the brain manufactures, facilitate communication across the dendrites.

Some neurons develop more elaborate connections with other neurons, while neurons that go unactivated are shed. It's a "use it" phenomenon, where neurons that the brain uses grow in complexity, while those that are inactive gradually disappear. Brain development and pruning are indicators of the brain's plasticity, where brains beings develop new neural connections over time and shed others in response to experiences. Infancy and early childhood are times for the greatest development and pruning of neurons.

Yet, parents who are at high risk to physically abuse their children will probably physically abuse even "easy" children. This affects children's brain development. These children eventually may become "difficult" in response to physical abuse. Parents at low risk to physically abuse children are unlikely to physically abuse "difficult" children, especially if they seek out supportive persons and educate themselves about their children's neurological conditions.

In summary, physical abuse of children affects the development of their brains. Further discussion of neurobiology are present later in this chapter as I discuss the other components of the NEATS.

Parents' Neurobiology

Understanding parents' possible neurological issues is important, too. If parents have autism spectrum disorders, fetal alcohol effects, or adult ADHD, the implications of these conditions for children's safety and for parents' capacities to respond to social services have to be explored. Neurological conditions of extended family members and friends of the family also is an important part of treatment planning because these other people not only can influence how parents deal with their children, but they could potentially provide alternative care if this becomes necessary.

Attachment

NEATS is spelled NEATS and not NAETS, but attachment is so closely linked to brain development that in the present discussion, I cover attachment after neurobiology. Attachment is defined as behaviors that maintain contact with care providers who serve as a secure base from which to explore and to which to return under times of stress, as well as to serve as a source of nurturance, love and affirmation. Attachment is also a process, whose outward characteristics change as children grow and develop, but at its core attachment relationships are a source of nurturance, problem-solving, affirmation, and even courage to try new things or to persist when times are tough. This definition is a slightly edited quote from the book *The NEATS: A Child & Family Assessment* (Gilgun, 2010).

Attachment relationships is a major part of the "experience/environment/nurture" side of gene-environment/nature-nurture interactions. Attachment and brain development do much more than shape neural networks. The combination of neurobiology and attachment also shapes how individuals experience and interpret the world and how they act upon the world, including how they interact with other people. Thinking, emotion, and actions are mediated through mental constructs called inner working models (IWM), schemas, or inner representations. Children are born with some IWMs, such as how to cry, seek nourishment, such and move arms and legs. Others arise through experience.

IWMs are internalizations of experiences and interpretations of experiences. They represent the kinds of interactions—or attachment relationships--that infants and children experience with their primary care providers. They are encoded in brain circuits and activate automatically in response to how individuals interpret particular situations. Inner working models encode human experiences and are road maps and expectations of the self, others, and how the world works. Self-concept, values, and any other perceptions, expectations, values, cognitions, and emotions eventually become encoded within brain circuits that in turn give rise to IWMs.

Children who experience interactions with parents as secure attachments develop secure inner working models, where they expect others to be respectful, courteous, and interested in them, as they are respectful, courteous, and interested in others. They have capacities to trust others, just as they learned their parents are trustworthy. These expectations and behaviors arise out of the sensitive responsiveness that is characteristic of secure child-caregiver attachment relationships.

Other characteristics of secure attachments are attunement, contingent responsiveness, and mutual regulation. This means that children and parents pay attention to the wishes of each other. They do not impose on each other, except to redirect unwanted behaviors, but enjoy the freely offered give and take between them. When children have enough interaction with parents, they signal through behavior and, when they are older, through words that they want a break. Parents who respect this kind of give and take are said to be attuned and contingently responsive. Parents engage with children and children engage with parents in mutually response ways.

Even the most secure relationships are not perfect. There are breakdowns in attunement, mutuality, and contingency. Feelings can be hurt and expectations not met on both sides. The result is a need for repair. Depending on age and developmental level, caregivers and children work out various ways to re-connect or repair their connections. As the children develop, parents and children talk through their differences and reconnect. Capacities to repair relationships after inevitable breakdowns are characteristic of secure relationships. Like other learnings, processes of repair are encoded in brain circuits and become part of IWMs.

Through trial and error children also learn that some other people may not be trustworthy. They talk things over with their trusted attachment figures and learn to cope with untrustworthy others. These learnings, too, are encoded in brain circuits and become part of their IWMs. Attachment relationships have many other aspects, and these are more fully covered in Gilgun (2010) and readings listed in the reference section.

Children who experience physical abuse are unlikely to have secure attachments with parents who abuse them. They are likely to develop inner working models of parents as untrustworthy. They may not learn about repair of relationships because parents do not attempt repair, nor do they respond to children's attempts at repair. The many subtle aspects of secure relationships may not develop within the IWMs of children who experience physical abuse, although capacities for repair may develop in fragmented and inconsistent ways.

The extent of the physical abuse, the capacities of parents to model and support repair in breakdowns, and parents' capacities for sensitive responsiveness shape the kinds of attachment styles and IWMs that children develop. Parents who have dismissive attachment styles usually raise children with avoidant attachment styles. Parents with dismissive styles may not believe that the physical actions they take against their children are abuse. They also may not believe that these actions harm children. If they believe they have not harmed their children, they will not initiate repair, nor will they respond to children's attempts at repair.

Children with avoidant attachments develop IWMs that guide them to evade interacting with caregivers and others in order to protect themselves from further hurt. The children often are sad and lonely and think of themselves as bad and worthless. They internalize how their parents have treated them. They may also encode beliefs that physical abuse is natural and normal. These beliefs are encoded on brain circuits and activate themselves automatically.

Children who have ambivalent or disorganized styles of attachment usually have parents with preoccupied or disorganized styles of adult attachments. If their parents physically abuse them, repair is unlikely, or if it happens, it is inconsistent, incomplete, not mutually contingent, and confusing. These children, like children with avoidant styles of attachment, are at risk to develop IWMs that encode mistrust of others. They may also develop beliefs that the world is not safe, that other people are not trustworthy, and that they are bad children. Like children with avoidant attachment styles and dismissive caregivers, children with ambivalent or disorganized attachment styles may encode beliefs that physical abuse is natural and normal.

Caregivers' attachment styles usually mirror the types of attachment they had with their own parents. Caregivers' IWMs therefore shape how they perceive their own parents' treatment of them and how they interpret the effects of their physical acts on their children.

Through therapy and introspection, individuals may be able to identity the types of IWMs they have developed. By becoming aware of their expectations of self, others, and how the world works, they may be able to change their IWMs, but this can be difficult, as worthwhile as such efforts are. Inflexible thinking styles are characteristic of persons with avoidant, ambivalent, or disorganized attachments and associated IWMs.

Persons in caregivers' and children's ecology, such as extended family, teachers, coaches, clergy, and friends' parents may influence children's IWMs. When parents are physically abusive, unable to initiate repair, and unable and/or unwilling to change their behaviors, these other people may be able to provide secure attachments that will help children build IWMs that encode trust, flexible thinking, and positive expectations. If children feel safe with people in these other ecologies, they may be able to do the kinds of repair that their parents were unable to do. Children require the safety of secure relationships to work through the effects of physical abuse, to modify their inner working models, and to strengthen IWMs that lead them to expect that some people are trustworthy and that they are not bad children but good children who have competencies. These issues are discussed in more detail in the section on trauma.

Service Provider Capacities

Many of the qualities of effective, reciprocal, and mutually contingent parenting are similar to qualities in effective working relationships that service providers and service users develop. Service providers can use these ideas to evaluate their own effectiveness. Key issues are whether service providers offer safety and security, build relationships with service providers, listen quietly and calmly as service users discuss issues that trouble them, help service users problem solve, and also be clear that some behaviors not only are not acceptable but are against the law, as child physical abuse is. They also offer guidance and referrals for service users as part of treatment plans that they develop in interactions with service users.

Understanding parents' attachment styles is inseparable from the assessment of children's attachment styles. Factors that might influence parents' capacities for attachment are important to identify and to assess. If, for example, parents have neurological issues such autism spectrum disorders, fetal alcohol effects, or adult ADHD, the conditions do not automatically rule out parents as secure attachment figures. If, however, parents have physically abused these children and they have neurological conditions, then case planning has to assess whether and how neurological conditions contributed to problematic attachment behaviors.

Neurological conditions and attachment styles of extended family members and friends of the family also is an important part of treatment planning because these other people not only can influence how parents deal with their children, but they could potentially provide alternative care if this becomes necessary.

Whether school personnel and other service providers show capacities related to secure attachment is another area to assess when doing treatment planning in cases of child physical abuse. The issue is whether these professionals are sensitively responsive to parents and children, set clear limits on hurtful behaviors, and offer resources that may help make things better for parents and children. In terms of setting clear limits, service providers may be agents of social control in that they have legal mandates to supervise parents who have physically abused their children. They can petition courts for a change of child custody if they have evidence that the parents have re-abused their children.

Executive Function

Executive function (EF) is a term that covers a broad range of capacities related to judgment, problem-solving, organization of self, anticipation of consequences, working memory, flexible thinking, and following rules and directions. Regulation of emotions, thoughts, and behaviors is part of executive function as well, but in the NEATS assessment, self-regulation is a separate category because of its significance in social work and other applied settings. This definition is a slight modification of a quote from Gilgun (2010).

Parents who physically abuse their children have issues with EF. They do not anticipate and may not take seriously the effects of physical abuse on children. The short-term gain of forcing compliance on children and also the pleasure they may take in physical strikes against children may overwhelm any thought about longer-term consequences for their children and for their relation-ships with their children. These parents also have poor problem-solving skills characterized by inability to use alternatives to physi-cal abuse, at least in some situations. They have limited abilities and/or limited opportunities to reflect on their own attachment histories with their parents. They operate through automatically activated schemas that they developed through hurtful and unex-amined interactions with their own parents. Widespread societal acceptance of violence as a means of solving problems reinforces their beliefs in the physical mistreatment of their children.

Ironically, parents who physically abuse their children may show some EF in terms of whom they chose to abuse and under what circumstances. They typically physically abuse children who are too small and weak to fight back. They often commit their abu-sive acts in private so as to avoid detection and possible arrest. They may tell their children not to talk about family business with outsiders. This shows that they think about the possibilities that the children will hurt them, that they know that they are doing something wrong and illegal, and that they find far enough ahead to be careful to ensure that they protect themselves against nega-tive consequences for their physical abuse.

Children who have experienced physical abuse also may have issues with EF, unless they have had opportunities to work through the effects of the abuse with trustworthy others. They, like their parents, may act without thinking of the consequences. If they believe that physical aggression is how they are supposed to act in situations of threat, they will do so. If they have learned to be avoidant of threatening situations, they will tend to withdraw from potentially threatening situations. They may misperceive situations to be threatening when they are not. Misperceptions are common in children who have experienced physical abuse and have not have opportunities to work through effects of physical abuse.

In summary, the types of attachment relationships children have experienced and their neurobiology influence the kinds of IWMs they have developed. Children with secure attachment styles typically have good EF. In most situations, they anticipate consequences, are sensitive to others, and follow rules. Human brains may not mature until the mid-twenties. Therefore, some issues with EF are expectable until that time, even for persons who have primarily experienced secure attachments. Most people have some issues with EF throughout their lives. After the brain has matured, deficits in EF have nothing to do with their age, but with how experiences and biology have shaped their brains.

Finally, it is important to assess the EF of other persons whom children come in contact, such as siblings, extended family members, teachers, clergy, neighbors, friends, and peers. Other persons in children's lives, adults as well as peers, not only can serve as attachment figures but can model good EF. As discussed previously, service providers may find persons who are part of extended family and friend networks may be capable of providing alternative care to children who have experienced physical abuse.

Service providers can assess themselves and other service providers in terms of their own EF. Do they make good judgments, base judgments upon a consideration a wide range of information, do they consider alternative responses, think flexibly, show empathy, and follow the rules?

Trauma

Trauma is an event that is life threatening or psychologically devastating to the point where persons' capacities to cope are overwhelmed. Any number of events may be traumatizing, including abuse and neglect, witnessing violence, death or other kind of loss of parents or siblings, abductions, car accidents, plane crashes, earthquakes, tidal waves, social dislocation, and war. Following trauma, individuals relive the traumatic event, fragmented memories related to the trauma arise unexpectedly, cognitive, emotional, and behavioral dysregulation occurs, and there is avoidance of reminders of the event. Trauma may change brain structures and become encoded in brain circuits related to memory and emotion. This is a direct quote from Gilgun (2010).

Child physical abuse is a trauma that affects children's sense of safety and well being. The traumatic event itself and the circumstances surrounding trauma are encoded in the brain. For example, if parents physically abuse their children with a yardstick in a particular room at Halloween, the children will store reminders of the event in their brains. Possible stored reminders are the yardstick, how the parents looked and what they said, decorations in the room, the kinds of candy or other treats for trick or treat, and any eerie Halloween sounds that parents may have piped into the room. The memories usually are storied as fragments. The fragments may become disconnected from the abuse itself, and children who have experienced physical abuse may not have conscious memories of these fragments. However, when children experience reminders of the abuse, such as Halloween decorations, memories of the abuse itself may surge into consciousness. Children then relive the abuse.

Since the fragmented memories may be disconnected from the trauma, children, parents, and other adults may be baffled as to what triggered the reliving of the trauma. Parents and other adults may even mistake trauma-linked behaviors for oppositional behaviors or for attention deficit-hyperactivity behaviors. If this happens they may respond punitively. Punitive responses are harmful. Not only do they foster mistrust, but they also add to children's experiences of traumatic memories.

Sometimes, children may avoid situations where they are afraid they will experience the reminders, or they may continually re-enact the traumatic event through play. Without adult intervention within the safety of secure relationships, children may stay stuck in their preoccupations and in their avoidances.

Two sites of the brain that are sensitive to trauma are the amygdala and the hippocampus. The amygdala are two almond-shaped structures on both sides of the brain about where ears are located. They are the sites of emotions. The hippocampus are two horse-shaped structures located on both sides of the brain and located near the amygdala. The hippocampus store memories, often as fragments. High degrees of stress may damage and even kill neurons in the hippocampus, which can affect storage of memories and could account for some fragmentation of memories.

The hippocampus matures later than the amygdala. Children may have no memories of traumatic events, but reminders of the trauma can trigger emotional responses encoded in the amygdala. Thus, children who experience physical abuse before the ages of four and five may have no or few memories of the abuse stored in the hippocampus, but they have emotional memories stored in the amygdala that can be triggered by reminders of the abuse.

When children relive traumatic memories, they typically experience a flooding of memories, thoughts, and emotions. This flood may stimulate the seeking of comfort from attachment figures, or lead to withdrawn, aggressive, or disorganized behaviors. In terms of brain function, their amygdalas are stimulated to activate emotional responses. These responses then trigger fragments of memories stored in the hippocampus. Memories activate themselves. Children then feel strong and confusions emotions and become caught up in traumatic memories. If they have had the safety of secure relationships to help them process trauma, they have developed neural pathways that lead to automatic activation of pathways in the prefrontal cortex, which is the seat of reasoning. Children who have developed neural pathways that lead directly to activation of pathways in the prefrontal cortex may experience dysregulation for a time because of activation of traumatic memories, but they also know to seek the safety and comfort of attachment figures. Thus a child frightened by a loud noise that might trigger traumatic memories, will run toward a nearby parent or some other persons with whom they feel safe. As children grow older, they develop other means of coping with dsyregulation, although the core of efforts to re-regulate prosocially is to seek comfort and safety, as will be discuss later in this chapter .

Children with avoidant, ambivalent, and disorganized styles of attachment that arise from dismissive, preoccupied, and disorganized parental attachment styles may have difficulties coping when traumatic memories activate themselves. They may become withdrawn and anxious, aggressive and hurtful to others, or mixture of withdrawal, aggression and self-destructive behaviors. While there are variations as to how individual children with various styles of attachment respond to trauma, these responses affect children's development. They require the safety of secure relationships so that they can slowly and at their own speed deal with the effects of trauma.

Parental Responses

Many parents and other care providers are unable to respond sensitively to children reliving trauma. They may not recognize children's behaviors as linked to trauma, or they may have styles of attachment that lead them to dismiss, become preoccupied, or act in contradictory ways in response to children's re-experiencing of trauma. These parents require, at a minimum, education about trauma and how to parent children who have experienced trauma. They and their children also benefit from emotional support in their efforts to be sensitively responsive to their children. Some parents may require therapy to deal with their own trauma, if their unattended traumas appear to interfere with their attunement to their children and their capacities to provide the warmth, safety, and structure that children require to recover from trauma.

Service Provider Responses

Service providers, too, must be emotionally available and attuned to parents and their traumatized children. To be effective, they require open-mindedness to the issues and their meanings. They have to maintain their own EF in order to provide or suggest services that fit the families to whom they provide services. Service providers must be willing to deal with biases and frustrations they may experience in their work with families where child physical abuse has appeared. Later in this chapter , I discuss the secondary trauma that service providers may experience and ways to deal with it. Bias and frustration can be a response to unattended secondary trauma, which is trauma that providers have not directly experienced but are responses to service user trauma.

Service providers also require expertise in building relationships with service users who have issues with trust. Parents may mistrust service providers because in the past they have experienced providers as sources of trauma. For instance, service providers in the past may have removed them from their homes and placed them in foster care. Service user mistrust is an obvious block to building relationships. If, however, treatment is to be effective, providers have to figure out how to form relationships with parents and their children, perhaps first by attempting to help parents to repair the past traumas they may have experienced at the hands of service providers.

Self-Regulation

Self-regulation is defined as capacities to manage and make sense of one's own thoughts, emotions, and behaviors in times of stress and in the course of everyday life. Self-regulation is often considered part of executive functions, but because of its centrality for children who have experienced children physical abuse and other traumas, the NEATS assessment treats self-regulation as it own category. Capacities for self-regulation are both genetic and experiential in origin. Subjectively, children experience dysregulation as a loss of control, of unmanageability of thoughts, emotions, and behaviors. Heart rate and breathing may become accelerated. This is a slightly edited quote from Gilgun (2010).

Dysregulation is uncomfortable and can be extremely painful emotionally. Children want to feel better; thus, they seek to re-regulate. Typically dysregulation occurs in response to the activation of memories associated with trauma. There are four general types of re-regulation: prosocial, antisocial, self-destructive, and inappropriate. Children who have relationships with attachment figures who provide the safety of secure relationships have a good chance of re-regulating in prosocial ways. If they experience physical abuse, they may dysregulate, but they are likely to have primarily prosocial responses. This means they will seek out attachment figures, look for comfort, and talk about what has happened. Attachment figures who provide the safety of secure relationships respond with empathy, allow children to process through their trauma, and will problem solve with the children to see how to respond to the effects of physical abuse and other traumas.

Children who do not have the safety of secure relationships may have more prolonged bouts of dysregulation. Some may attempt to re-regulate in antisocial ways. In other words, they may attempt is to make themselves feel better through physical aggression and destruction of property, as previously discussed. Adults may think these kinds of dysregulations are signs of oppositional behaviors or even conduct disorders. They could be, but if children get the help they require, many of these antisocial behaviors might not occur. Antisocial responses are associated with ambivalent and disorganized styles of child attachment and dismissive, preoccupied, and disorganized parental attachments. Children who dysregulate in this way may have co-existing neurological conditions. A competent neurological evaluation might bring clarity to these issues.

Children may also seek to re-regulate through self-harm. They may cut themselves, drink alcohol, take drugs, or over-eat. Still others may engage in inappropriate activities, such as sexual preoccupations or preoccupations with violent video games, or simply tune people out. Tuning people out can be symptoms of co-occurring neurological conditions such as attention deficit disorders or petit mal seizures, but they could also be signs of trauma.

Service Provider Issues

Service providers have an important role to play when children and parents have issues with self-regulation. They must have training to recognize dysregulation, and they must have capacities to keep themselves regulated. Sometimes they dysregulations and the traumas associated with them trigger secondary trauma in providers. In these cases, providers must have capacities for maintaining their cognitive and emotional balance while with service users. They can have their own "melt-downs" later.

When doing a NEATS assessment, service providers assess parents, other attachment figures, and other persons who deal with the children such as teachers and coaches, for their styles of self-regulation and re-regulation. In order for children to learn to re-regulate prosocially, the adults who spend time with children must also regulate themselves prosocially. If they do not, then in order to help children with the effects of physical abuse, they must do whatever it takes to learn to self-regulate prosocially. The more children have been exposed to prosocial means of self-regulation and re-regulation and the more children's attachment figures offer safety and security, the more likely children who have experienced physical abuse will recover and will re-regulate in the future through prosocial means.

Service providers have important roles in developing plans to help children, their parents, and other persons who are in contact with children to learn about self-regulation, dysregulation, and re-regulation. While providers may or may not use the exact terms that I use in describing these issues, their understanding of the issues and their expertise in knowing how to respond will greatly enhance their effectiveness.

Characteristics of Helpful Interventions

Principles drawn from the NEATS can be useful in planning, developing, and evaluating treatment plans, programs meant to rebuild family relationships after physical abuse, and programs whose purpose is the prevention of child physical abuse. In addition, service providers can use these principles to evaluate themselves and the quality of service provision itself. The NEATS can also be helpful in service provider self-evaluation and evaluation of the quality of services. The promotion of healthy relationships is a key issue in effective service provision. Helpful self-evaluations and evaluation of programs and policies center around issues of relationships. To the extent that service providers, programs, and policies are successful in promoting healthy relationships, these interventions succeed.

Service Provider Self-Evaluation

Work with children and families where child physical abuse has occurred is hard on service providers. Seeing a battered, bruised child with eyes swollen shut, their faces full of the pain of trauma, and their bodies tense with shock can lead to secondary trauma in service providers. Listening to service users talk about their experiences of physical abuse and other traumas can also lead to secondary trauma, which is sometimes called vicarious trauma. It's a good idea for service providers to do periodic self-evaluations along the lines of the NEATS to ensure that they are capable of building helpful relationships with clients and that they are maintaining their own emotional and physical health.

Secondary trauma arises when life events that service providers have not experienced directly but have witnessed overwhelm their usual coping capacities. Service providers know they have experienced secondary trauma when thoughts and images of the trauma they witnesses rise into awareness seemingly on their own. When providers experience these intrusive thoughts and images, they are at risk to be distracted by them and to be irritable and upset. Their sleep may be disturbed, adding to irritability. The irritability may spill over into personal and professional relations. Sometimes providers also avoid reminders of the event.

These responses may interfere with effectiveness in terms of capacities for thinking and concentration. They may also affect sensitive responsiveness to others, which in turn affects relationships. If providers do not consciously and conscientiously deal with their secondary trauma, they may become depressed, anxious, and burned out. These conditions not only affect quality of services they provide but also quality of personal life.

The following is a brief analysis of secondary trauma based on principles I drew from the NEATS.

Secondary trauma affects all five areas of the NEATS.

Neurobiology. Secondary trauma, like any other experience, stimulates the development of connections between neurons. The more frequently providers experience secondary trauma, the stronger the connection grow. Neural networks and their associated inner working models may become more easily activated as time goes on in the relative absence of IWMs that offset these effects. Secondary trauma can arise simply because of the horrific nature of the trauma. Any compassionate human being is at risk of experiencing secondary trauma, regardless of their own trauma histories. Often, however, service users, like any other human beings, have experienced personal traumas. Secondary trauma can activate memories of earlier traumas. This threatens capacities for effectiveness both professionally and personally.

In response to secondary trauma, neural pathways associated with help-seeking and positive coping may be activated. Service providers then engage in a large range of positive behaviors that will lead to coping with, adapting to, and overcoming the effects of secondary trauma. In other words, they will engage in activities that lead to resilience. In these cases, service providers may develop increased capacities for coping with secondary trauma and for remaining effective when confronted with the difficult life events of others.

Active and successful coping with secondary trauma will stimulate the growth and development of neural pathways and associated IWMs that build service user capacities to deal with events that might otherwise lead to secondary trauma. Service users might also develop increased capacities to cope with previous trauma.

If service providers cannot activate strategies that help them cope, they are at risk to engage in self-destructive, self-defeating, and aggression ways of dealing with dysregulations associated with secondary trauma. For example, they may engage in thrill-seeking behaviors that stimulate the release of neurotransmitters that temporarily life mood. These behaviors include the use of cocaine and other drugs, reckless driving, and gambling. They may be irritable and insensitive to co-workers, service users, and their own families.

Executive function. Service providers who are overwhelmed with the effects of secondary trauma, including the reactivation of personal traumas, may not have good judgment, may be unable to experience empathy for themselves and others, and may be at risk to act out the irritability and upset that they feel. Some service providers become depressed and anxious. These emotional states can lead to further insensitivity to others, while at the same time they experience suffering and emotional pain. Their have poor judgment that can lead to abuse of chemicals, inappropriate relationships with clients, or other self-defeating and hurtful strategies. These responses threaten and sometimes undermine their capacities for maintaining and promoting healthy relationships.

Service providers also are at risk to think in rigid ways and assume that how they cope with their own personal trauma is the way that service users should cope as well. They may impose their views on service providers without doing a full NEATS assessment that brings different kinds of important information into the open.

On the other hand, service providers may be able to dig deep and connect with values such as justice, care, and respect for the autonomy of others and respect for themselves. These healthy beliefs will immediately challenge any thoughts of being irritable and unkind, or of imposing their wills on others. Concern for their own well-being and the recognition that any depression and anxiety they experience may have negative effects on others will also challenge the inner working models that cut them off from connections to others.

Attachment and Trauma. Service providers who experience secondary trauma may cope through talking over the meanings of these traumas with trusted others. Once again the centrality of relationships is evident. The trusted others may be supervisors, co-workers, members of professional support groups, clergy, or therapists. Sometimes the memories that surface are personal enough and sensitive that service providers first share them with therapists who have specialized training in trauma work.

Often, the effects of secondary trauma can overburden personal relationships. As a result, it's often wise for service providers not to attempt to work through the effects of secondary trauma with spouses, significant others, and friends. They may mention some of the effects and share the difficulties, but for the processing through, I have found that other professionals are more equipped than personal friends and family. Friends and family may also be traumatized by the stories service providers tell. Such situations can be knotty and difficult to unravel. Professionals are better equipped to deal with service providers' secondary and primary traumas.

Self-Regulation. Service user dysregulation is inevitable in work with children who have experienced physical abuse. It is important for service users to know when they are dysregulated and then to seek to re-regulate in prosocial ways. The experience of secondary trauma can feel like being dropped in boiling oil, can be flooding of emotions such as anxiety and anger, and show itself through difficulty breathing, headaches and other bodily symptoms. The signs are hard to miss, but service providers may not know at first what is going on and what to do about these reactions.

To keep themselves regulated, service providers engage in a variety of behaviors, including those already discussed, such as seek out attachment figures and process through the meanings of secondary trauma and any personal trauma now activated. Vigilance about inappropriate and hurtful ways to self-regulate is important. Examples of inappropriate means of self-regulations include those already mentioned and others, such as chemical use, risky, thrill-seeking behaviors, and using service users to satisfy own needs, such as sexual relations with clients or treating clients as friends and confidants.

There are many ways to maintain self-regulation, but the key strategy is honesty. This means a direct look at and grappling with the meanings of secondary trauma and any associated primary trauma. Service users first learn this honesty within the safety of secure family relationships. At least one person who influenced them will have been capable of emotional honesty, which service providers learn to emulate. With these capacities, seeking others to process difficult events becomes second nature.

Other strategies for self-regulation also can be helpful, such as vigorous physical exercise that discharges negative energy and may stimulate calming neurotransmitters, engaging in enjoyable activities such as singing, dancing, and watching funny movies. Some providers find journaling, talking into tape recorders, yoga, and meditation are helpful. Doing something for someone else, such as checking in on a relative, doing something for a neighbor, friend, or family member, or volunteering at a charitable organization can be helpful. These strategies fall into three main categories: direct discharge of emotions, moving away from disturbing thoughts and emotions, and grappling with and dealing directly with the disturbing memories, emotions, and thoughts. In combination, these three general types of strategies will lead to prosocial re-regulation and increased capacities for self-regulation.

There are rewards for engaging in these self-regulatory strategies. As providers become familiar with our own painful emotions and memories, they are more able to cope with them. Coping well frees energy and attention for other interests. Some people who cope well find they have an increased capacity to form relationships with others, set limits on the behaviors of others, and enjoy theatre, music, and other arts. Some even take up new hobbies and find more satisfaction not only in hobbies but in many other aspects of their lives. Their competence in personal and professional relationships may be enhanced.

Principles for Evaluating Services, Programs, and Policies

The NEATS can be a source of principles for the evaluation of services, programs, and policies. The central issue with the NEATS is relationships in ecological and developmental perspectives. Supportive relationships are nested. They exist in families and between family members. They exist between family members and supportive networks of family, friends, and community groups and agencies. They are based upon histories of being part of supportive secure relationships across these various networks. Neurological conditions and trauma can affect quality of relationships. If parents receive the support and education that often is necessary to parent children with neurological conditions and/or trauma, then all will be well for them.

Insecure attachment arise when parents have experienced trauma that has gone unattended and if they have unmanaged neurological conditions. In short, they have not had the safety of secure relationships to work through their trauma nor have they had adequate care to learn how to manage their neurological conditions. Some parents have experienced complex traumas that complicates recovery even further. The IWMs that parents develop arise out of interactions between experience and genetics. If parents have experienced physical abuse themselves and have witnessed physical abuse in their families, communities, and elsewhere, they are at high risk to develop powerful IWMs that may predispose them to self-regulate in antisocial ways or simply to chose to be violent to get what they want even when they are regulated.

Service providers and networks of social services have a major task to understand service users' IWMs and how these IWMs lead to behaviors that harm their children or that promote children's well being and development. Service providers can understand IWMs through conversations where they observe parental beliefs. They can also observe parents' behaviors to get an idea of what parents believe.

Understanding and working with beliefs and the consequences of actions are difficult. Understanding the centrality of beliefs and actions in working with children and families who have experienced physical abuse is a necessary part of program and policy effectiveness.

In short, optimal human development takes place within the safety of secure relationships within families. How well families function depends upon secure relationships with extended families and others who are part of extended networks, both in the present and the past. These principles are abstract and general. Yet, they are the foundation of evaluations of services, programs, and policies. The following are guidelines for evaluation.

Do services, programs, and policies do the following? If they do, how do they do them?

1. They promote secure attachments between parents and children, between parents, and between parents and children and other members of social networks with whom they have contact;
2. They identify issues that interfere with secure attachments;
   a. Primary among these issues are beliefs: what parents believe about their roles as parent and how they are supposed to raise their children; what they believe about the physical abuse of children; what they believe about how they treat their children; whether they are willing to do whatever it takes to ensure that their children receive the care they require to develop well;
   b. Whether basic human needs for safety, food, clothing, shelter, and medical care are met;
3. They provide services and other experiences that help parents and children to cope with, adapt to, or overcome the issues that interfere with secure attachments;
   a. These services include education, parent support groups, mental health and chemical dependency

treatment when needed; parents own therapy to deal with their own unattended traumas; early childhood family education; infant mental health services; medical care

4. They support services providers so that service providers have competence in the areas in which they do their practice;

    a. Agencies provide training and resources that support service providers' work;

    b. They support and encourage service providers

        i. to evaluate themselves and their competencies;

        ii. to develop capacities for behaving in ways consistent with secure attachments:

            1. attunement;

            2. serve as a place of safety and security;

            3. clear expectations;

            4. set limits;

            5. recognize prosocial behaviors;

        iii. to take good care of themselves, especially in terms of dealing with secondary trauma

        iv. to develop skills to build relationships with service users who might have issues with neurobiology, executive function, attachment, trauma, and self-regulation;

5. The social service network has resources to support and promote secure attachments in families.

Discussion

A NEATS analysis of child physical abuse directs attention to important areas for service providers to assess and then to address in treatment plans. This chapter focuses primarily on assessment. Chapter 14 shows how NEATS assessment can guide the development of treatment plans.

The central issue is to assess whether children have families that can provide the safety of secure relationships and whether secure relationships are available to children in other social networks.

When children have secure relationships, there is hope that they can learn to cope with adapt to and overcome the effects of physical abuse and other traumas. Often parents and others important to children have unattended issues related to attachment, beliefs, executive function, trauma, and self-regulation that interfere with their capacities for providing the safety of secure relationships. They may also have unattended neurological issues.

In these cases, service providers, in collaboration with parents and children, develop strategies for promoting secure relationships and for dealing directly with issues that interfere with the development of secure relationships. Success happens when service users and service providers develop collaborative relationships within networks of supportive social networks and social services.

Most children whose parents have physically abused them remain in the home. Social services are involved with them and their families. Sometimes services make a difference for children and their families and sometimes they do not. This is a fact that many providers find difficult, but it is a fact nonetheless.

Effective service provision depends upon the competence of service providers, the network of services that are available to children and families, and child and family willingness to engage with service providers. Service provider competence is part of effective services. Providers have little control over agency policies and resources that agencies offer. Enlightened policies promote programs that are responsive to what families and children need to develop optimally. Many children and families benefit from current policies and programs. Some do not.

In summary, the NEATS provides practice principles that show the importance of the promotion of secure relationships and of dealing with issues that interfere with the development and maintenance of secure relationship. In addition, promotion of secure family relationships requires the support of other social networks. These are difficult tasks.

References

Berk, Laura E. (2008). *Child development* (8th ed.). Boston: Allyn and Bacon.

Bride, Brian E. (2007). Prevalence of secondary traumatic stress among social workers. *Social Work, 52(1)*, 63-70.

Clark, Roseanne, Audrey Tluczek, & Roger Brown (2008) A mother-infant therapy group model for postpartum depression. *Infant Mental Health Journal,* 29(5), 514-536.

Davies, Douglas (2011). *Child Development: A practitioner's guide (3rd ed.).* New York: Guilford.

Gilgun, Jane F. (2009). Secondary trauma as an occupational hazard of social service providers. Available on Amazon Kindle and scribd.com at http://www.scribd.com/doc/23517922/Secondary-Trauma-as-an-Occupational-Hazard-for-Social-Service-Professionals/

Gilgun, Jane F. (2010). *The NEATS: A Child & Family Assessment.* Available on Amazon Kindle, iBooks, & scribd.com at http://www.scribd.com/doc/16496944/The-NEATS-A-Child-Family-Assessment/

Hinshaw-Fusilier, Sarah, Neil W. Boris, & Charles H. Neanah (1999). Reactive attachment disorder in maltreated twins. *Infant Mental Health Journal, 20(1),* 42-59.

Kidd, Sue Monk (2002). *The secret life of bees.* New York: Penguin.

Lieberman, Alicia F. (2004). Traumatic stress and quality of attachment: Reality and internalization in disorders of infant mental health. *Infant Mental Health Journal, 25(4),* 336-351.

Lederman, Cindy S, Joy D. Osofsky, & Lynne Katz (2007). When the bough breaks the cradle will fall: Promoting the health and well-being of infants and toddlers in juvenile court. *Infant Mental Health Journal, 28(4)*, 440-448.

Miller-Perrin, C.L. & Perrin R.D. (2007). *Child maltreatment: An introduction.* (2nd ed.). Sage: Thousand Oaks, CA.

Teicher, Martin H. (2002). Scars that won't heal: The neurobiology of child abuse: Maltreatment at an early age can have enduring negative effects on a child's brain. *Scientific American, 286(3)*, 68-76.

The United Nations Convention of the Rights of the Child. Available through an internet search.

Weatherson, Deborah J., Julie Ribaudo, & Sandra Glovak (2002). Becoming whole: Combining infant mental health and occupational therapy on behalf of a toddler with sensory integration difficulties and his family. *Infants and Young Children, 15(1)*, 19-28.

Rutter, Michael (2006). Autism: Its recognition, early diagnosis, and service implications. *Journal of Developmental and Behavioral Pediatrics, 27 (Suppl.)*, S54-S58.

Weatherson, Deborah J., Julie Ribaudo, & Sandra Glovak (2002). Becoming whole: Combining infant mental health and occupational therapy on behalf of a toddler with sensory integration difficulties and his family. *Infants and Young Children, 15(1)*, 19-27.

Winter, Karen. (2010). The perspectives of young children in care about their circumstances and implications for social work practice. *Child and Family Social Work, 15*, 186-195.

13

A NEATS Analysis
of Children with Sexual Behavior Issues

hildren show many different kinds of sexual behaviors.
These behaviors range from developmentally appropriate
to exploitive and aggressive acts that harm others, almost
always other children. In this chapter, I discuss the varieties
of children's sexual behaviors using three kinds of assessments.
They are the Gil and Johnson typology, the NEATS, which is a
child and family assessment that I developed, and ideas from research on resilience and risk.

Through the use of these assessments, I build understandings of the complex issues involved in children's sexual
development. I also provide guidelines for how adults can respond
so that children develop to their optimal potential. Too often parents and other adults do not know what to do. Their attempts to
help sometimes are effective and sometimes not. Concerned adults
may make things worse. This chapter provides information that
will help parents and others make informed decisions about how to
respond to children's sexual behaviors.

The types of childhood sexual behaviors that I discuss are
developmentally appropriate, inappropriate sexual exploration,
abuse reactive sexual behaviors, extensive mutual sexual behaviors,
and molesting behaviors that children commit. By children, I mean
young people 12 and younger. These categories are based upon the

work of Eliana Gil and Toni Johnson. I have done long-term research on the development of violent behaviors and use my own
research and understandings in this chapter as well as ideas from
Gil and Johnson.

Developmentally Appropriate Sexual Behaviors

Children's sexual development begins before birth. Studies
of fetal development in the womb show that girl fetuses experience
genital swelling and boy fetuses have erections. This is nature's way
of ensuring healthy development, just as fetal kicking signals physical development.

From an early age, children enjoy touching their genitals.
Parents know well that when they bathe young children, it's not
unusual for children's hands to go directly to their genitals. Little
boys may run around naked to show off their erections. Some say,
"Look. My penis is standing up." Running around naked is an activity that preschoolers enjoy.

Most children take pleasure in touching their genitals. Early
in their lives, parents teach young children when and where such
touch is appropriate and when it is not. This is an example of what
parents and others, such as day care providers, can say, when children touch their genitals in public.

> *I know it feels good to touch your penis/vulva. This kind of behavior
> is private. That means you do not touch your vulva/penis when other
> people are around. You can touch yourself in your own bedroom or
> when you take a bath or shower and you are by yourself.*

Sometimes parents or other adults find children undressed
and inspecting each others' genitals. When adults are taken by sur-
prise, it's okay to take a minute or two to think about how to
handle this. Then adults can walk into the area where the children
are and say something like the following.

I see you are curious about what girls and/or boys look like.[The adult pauses to allow the children to respond.] *I want you to get dressed now.*

Then you and I can talk about the sexual body parts of boys and girls. I have a book called A Very Touching Book *that I think you will like. We'll read it together. Then you can read it whenever you want. You can talk to me about sex any time you want.*

As children grow older, they continue to engage in behaviors that are related to sexuality. They wonder about where babies come from. They often have boyfriends and girlfriends even as young children, and they may find sexual terms and jokes hilarious. Some elementary school teachers find fourth graders to be the most foul-mouthed of all people they have known. They laugh in the teachers' room about what they overhear students say to each other.

As children enter teen years, they may hug and kiss each other. Some may touch each other sexually. Group masturbation sometimes occurs. As children mature toward adulthood, their sexual behaviors become more focused on sexual pleasure and hopefully also on mutual respect.

When sexual development is appropriate, sexuality is one of many interests that children and young people have. They have many other interests, such as sports, school, hobbies, hanging out with friends, and volunteer work. Each area of development requires parental guidance, nurturing, and encouragement.

Inappropriate Sexual Exploration

Without realizing what they are doing, some children may cross the line and take advantage of other children out of sexual curiosity. An example is Charlie, an eight year-old boy who told four year-old Alexa to pull down her pants and then touched the child's genitals, including poking into her vagina. Alexa told her parents who told Charlie's parents. The parents asked Charlie about what he did. He told them. The parents said.

We don't want you to do this. Alexa is a lot younger than you. You probably didn't realize that this behavior is wrong.

Charlie immediately said he is sorry and won't do it again. He explained to his parents that he had been wondering what girls look like. When he was alone with Alexa, he decided to find out.

The parents said

We know you didn't know it is wrong. Now you do. We want you to tell Alexa you are sorry, and you won't do it again. Now you and I can talk about sex. You obviously want to know about it. We're sorry we haven't talked to you about sex more than we have. We can talk any time you want. If you don't bring up topics about sex for a while, we will.

Both Charlie and his parents did exactly what they said they would do. Charlie apologized to Alexa. She told him she didn't like what he did, and she didn't want him to do it again. Her parents asked her if she is afraid of Charlie. Alexa said, "No. He's nice to me." Charlie and Alexa lived on the same block but they didn't play together. Both children had friends their own age. They saw each other at the bus stop and the community center.

After the apology, both children were cautious when they saw each other. The parents continued to have short conversations with their children about the incident. Both were willing to meet together again as families if necessary for the children's well-being. They did not because they saw that the children resumed their casual relationship with each other.

Secure Attachments

Charlie and his family had what professionals call secure relationships. Charlie trusted his parents and his parents trusted him.

Ever since he was born, Charlie's parents have been there for him. They fed his when he was hungry and responded well to any distress he experienced. They played with him and respected his cues that he had had enough. They were contingently responsive. As he grew older, they helped him to express his emotions and want appropriately and helped him to learn that sometimes he had to wait for something he wanted.

They had the qualities associated with secure attachments: sensitive responsiveness, emotional availability, setting of limits, and showing Charlie how to behave in appropriate ways.

Charlie came to believe that he is a trustworthy person whom other people care about. He gradually internalized how his parents and other care providers treated him. He became a trustworthy and trusting human being.

Alexa's parents, too, provided Alexa with secure attachments that helped her as she worked through the effects of Charlie's behavior. In fact, she trusted her parents in new ways because of how they handled her fright about Charlie's sexual aggression.

Charlie was not perfect. His sexual behaviors with Alexa were inappropriate. His parents were not perfect. They could have done a more adequate job of educating Charlie about sexuality and respect for the personal boundaries of others. Charlie and his parents made mistakes, but they took responsibility for their mistakes, admitted when they were wrong, and took steps not to repeat their mistakes.

Protective Processes

When children have secure attachments, they have built-in protective factors. This means they develop capacities to cope with, adapt to, and overcome adversities. In Charlie's case, he had internalized trust of his parents, capacities to admit mistakes, and desires to be accountable. These protective factors were the foundation of his sense of being sorry over doing something that hurt Alexa, his willingness to apologize, and his openness to his parents' offer to talking with him about sexuality.

Charlie's parents showed they had internalized protective factors, too. They held Charlie accountable. They guided him toward appropriate behaviors, and they took responsibility for their inadequate sex education of Charlie.

In Alexa's case, she, too, had internalized trust of her parents. She told them right away about the abuse. They responded sensitively to her. They also contacted Charlie's parents to let them know. They did not want Charlie's parents to punish him, but to tell him not to do it again and explain why. They knew Charlie and his family well enough to trust that they would handle Charlie's behavior in ways that would not harm Charlie. They were willing to prepare Alexa to talk to Charlie about the abuse, which they did. They trusted that Charlie's parents would prepare Charlie, which they did.

Both sets of families and children showed the kinds of behaviors associated with secure attachments.

A NEATS Assessment

When children have secure attachments within their families, they typically have optimal neurological functioning, good executive skills, proscocial styles of self-regulation, and have the safety of secure relationships where they can process their experiences, including the effects of any trauma they have undergone. These five areas of functioning comprise the NEATS, which stands for **N**eurobiology, **E**xecutive Function, **A**ttachment, **T**rauma, and **S**elf-Regulation. The five parts of the NEATS assessment are connected. If children have secure attachments, they typically develop well in the other four areas. If there are issues with one area, then there may be issues in the other areas.

Neurobiology has to do with brain development. Charlie showed evidence of good neurological functioning because he understood what he had done, was appropriately sorry, and did not react emotionally to the point where he could not understand what he done. In other words, he had good executive function and self-regulation because, although he felt stressed, he was able to understand what he did was wrong, and he did what he needed to do to make up for his harmful behaviors.

Telling Alexa to pull her pants down and then penetrating her with his fingers shows poor executive function and the impulsivity that is part of issues with self-regulation. He did not think about the effects of this behavior on Alexa, on himself, on his family and on Alexa's family. He only thought to satisfy his own curiosity. This is tunnel vision characteristic of poor executive functions. Behaviorally, he violated another child's personal space and acted disrespectfully. This shows a lack of imagination and empathy that are also part of poor executive skills.

Fortunately, his parents and Alexa's had good executive function and self-regulation. They responded appropriately. They set limits on Charlie's behaviors, told him his behaviors were wrong, and guided him on how to make up for what he had done. His parents also realized that they needed to provide Charlie with more information about sexuality. These behaviors indicate good executive function.

The experience may have been difficult for Charlie. He may not have experienced trauma, which are life events that overwhelm children's capacities for coping with, adapting to, or overcoming trauma. Charlie's trauma would have been related to events surrounding responses to his inappropriate behaviors.

Children with trauma may have several behavioral and emotional effects. These include intrusive recall of memories related to the trauma, nightmares, fear and avoidance of reminders of the trauma, difficulty with self-regulation or mood swings, preoccupation with the trauma, and repetive re-enactment of the trauma.

Charlie was unlikely to have experienced trauma when his behaviors become known. His parents provided the safety and security required to work through stressful life events.

Alexa could have experienced trauma. Certainly she was frightened when she turned to her parents who provided her with a safe haven, where she worked through the effects of Charlie's abusive behaviors.

Worst Case Scenario

Had the police arrested Charlie, taken him from school in handcuffs, put him in jail cell, and then called his parents, Charlie would have been traumatized. Police have done this to young children. Such actions may have set Charlie back. Therefore, his apology to Alexa could have been delayed for weeks and months. The delay would have hurt Alexa.

If Charlie had received this treatment, Alexa may have blamed herself, which would have compounded the effects of Charlie's abusive behaviors. With the kinds of parents she had, Alexa is likely to have worked through the effects of both experiences.

Charlie and his parents had secure attachments. They would have been there for Charlie, and he may have worked through the trauma of police involvement. In addition, his parents would probably have sought professional help in this situation. They may not have been able to cope well without the help of others. Being as well put together as they were, they would have realized they needed the wisdom and guidance of professionals.

Parents who provide their children with secure attachments know their own limits and welcome the help of others.

Even without police involvement, well put together parents like Charlie's and Alexa's often seek professional consultation. They view professionals as possibly helpful to them, both in terms of educating them about children's sexual behaviors but also for providing them with emotional support and guidance during a difficult time in their lives.

Problematic Sexual Behaviors

An indicator of whether children's sexual behaviors are problematic is whether they stop the behaviors when parents ask them to and when parents explain when and where sexual behaviors are appropriate and inappropriate.

If children do not stop their behaviors, parents require consultation with knowledgeable professionals. The next three types of childhood sexual behaviors require parents and children to work cooperatively with professionals.

Sexually Abuse Reactive Childhood Behaviors

Some children behave in sexual ways as a means of coping with sexual trauma or other kinds of trauma. These are children with sexualized behaviors. They may masturbate in public, keep a stash of sexually explicit material, think about sexual things for much of the day, peep on persons who are in various stages of undress, or expose their sexual body parts.

While they often do not, some children with sexualized behaviors may also engage in sexual behaviors with other children. In their sexual behaviors, however, they do not force or trick other children. They persuade other children with no false promises or threats.

Many children show sexualized behaviors. Parents and other adults know that children have issues that require professional attention when parents ask the children to stop the behaviors, explain alternatives, and the behaviors continue. Some children may stop, but they and their may still benefit from professional attention in some situations.

Whenparents see their children act in sexualized ways and do not stop the behaviors after being asked to, parents may wonder if someone has sexually abused their children. They can gently ask if anyone has behaved that way with them. This is an example

I see that you enjoy touching your penis/vagina/looking at pictures of people with no clothes on. Has anyone done this with you?

Parents have to prepare themselves for the answers. Typically, abusers are people parents know and trust. It's terrible for parents when they find their children have experienced sexual abuse. They may be shocked and devastated when life partners or close relatives are the abusers.

Many children who have sexualized behaviors have experienced child sexual abuse. Gil and Johnson believe that these behaviors are reactions to being sexually abused. The younger children are when they are sexually abused, the more likely they are to develop sexualized behaviors.

A Case Study

Here is an example of a child who had sexualized behaviors and then stopped. Josie at four had experienced sexual abuse by her father a few times when she was between the ages of three and four. Within a few months after the abuse began, she began to stuff wet toilet paper into her vagina. She enjoyed how that felt. She also rubbed her vulva against her Teddy bear.

One morning, her mother saw her stuffing the toilet paper into her vagina. Her mother asked her to stop. Josie did. She also stopped rubbing herself with her toy bear. Josie did not have professional help for these behaviors. Her mother told her father about Josie's behaviors. Josie's father stopped molesting her, although he never told his wife what he had done.

Josie forgot all about her sexualized behaviors until she was in her forties. Her mother was dying of breast cancer. Her father had died about ten years earlier. Josie's mother told Josie about her sexualized behaviors when she was young. Josie felt a shiver of recognition. She had vague memories of her father's abuse and her sexualized behaviors. She never felt as if this early experience of abuse had harmed her sexual responses. She enjoyed sex and was happily married.

Josie told her mother how grateful she was that her mother talked to her about these behaviors. She assured her mother that she had had therapy and had no residual effects from the early sexualized behaviors. Josie believed her mother felt guilty, and that she, Josie, had eased her mother's guilt.

Josie came from a fairly well put-together family where she felt valued and loved. Her relationship with her father had been rocky, but she felt validated about her relationships with him because her mother and siblings agreed that her father was difficult. As a young adult, Josie had therapy to help her work out her guilt and rage toward her father. The therapy appeared to free her to fall in love and maintain good relationships with her husband and children. She had an excellent education and a good job. Overall, she had high life satisfaction.

A NEATS Analysis

A NEATS analysis shows that Josie had a secure relationship with her mother and with her siblings, but an ambivalent relationship with her father. She argued with her father a lot. Fortunately, he tolerated her resistance to his often autocratic rule. Their arguments probably helped her to maintain some semblance of trust in him and some sense of herself as someone who can stand up for herself.

There is evidence for Josie's good neurological functioning and for others in her family. Her father may have had some sort of neurological issues, perhaps a low grade form of bipolar disorder called cyclothymia. He had mood swings that Josie sound unnerving. That is why she argued with him. Two of her father's cousins

163

and one of his uncles had a diagnosis of bipolar disorder, lending further evidence that her father may have had neurological issues.

On the whole, Josie had secure attachments, good self-regulation, good executive function, and a lack of debilitating trauma. Her family lived in the same house in the same town with adequate income throughout her childhood and teenage years.

The protective factors in her life outweighed the risks.

Some children have sexualized behaviors, and they have not experienced sexual abuse. They became sexualized through exposure to the sexual behaviors of others. If their sexualized behaviors become resistant to change, they are like to have several risks in their lives and no one with whom they have secure attachments. If they had secure attachments, they would have had the safety children require to work through the effects of adverse life events.

Marty: A Case of No Sexual Abuse but Sexualized Behaviors

Marty's story shows that some children have sexualized behaviors but no known history of sexual abuse. Marty remembered his childhood as painful to the extreme. He experienced severe anxiety and fear of his parents. One of the last of several children, he reported that his parents not only beat him and verbally abused him, but they also neglected him emotionally and psychologically. He did not experience his parents as there for him.

In terms of the NEATS, he had an insecure style of attachment with his parents. He did not feel close to his siblings. They, therefore, did not provide him with the safety of secure relationships, either. On his own to deal with the many difficulties he faced, he was unable to develop good executive skills and self-regulation in regard to his anxieties.

Marty used to peek in on his older siblings having sex with their girlfriends and boyfriends. He found this sexually stimulating.

He masturbated while watching them. He began this behavior at eight. Within a short time, he found that when he masturbated. He felt a lot better. He masturbated whenever he felt anxiety in order to feel better. He masturbated several times a day to the point where he had sores on his penis.

Marty had a lot of anxiety. His masturbation was an attempt at self-soothing. Soothing through masturbation several times a day shows that Marty had issues with self-regulation and with executive function. He regulated his emotions through masturbation and not through turning to attachment figures to soothe him and to help him develop alternative behaviors to masturbation.

One of the characteristics of executive function is the capacity to find life-affirming solutions to difficult situations. Marty had no one to help him develop his executive skills. He was too young to develop them without the help of adults.

Marty had experienced many traumas in his life related to physical and emotional abuse and neglect. He had not experienced sexual abuse.

His parents had issues with attachment, executive function, and self-regulation. They may have had unattended traumas that interfered with their capacities for attachment. They may have had preoccupied styles of attachment that led them to ignore Marty and to be abusive and neglectful. They did not provide their son with the safety of secure relationships where he could develop a sense of himself as a trustworthy, worthy person with capacities for trusting others and for good executive skills and capacities for self-regulation.

Marty had sexual behavior issues, but he did not sexually abuse children until he became a father himself and his daughter was 12 years old. In his teenage years, he did peep into the bedroom windows of girls he wanted to have sex with. He also masturbated to fantasies about having sex with these girls as he watched them get ready for bed. He told himself

Hah. They think they are too good for me. I'm having sex with them anyway. They just don't know it.

That's how real his fantasies were to him.

In terms of risk and protective factors, Marty's risks far outweighed his protective factors. His own family was the setting for his risks and lack of protective factors.

Marty's family is the type of family that is unlikely to engage with professionals to help their children with sexual behavior issues. They may have dismissed the behaviors as trivial and refused professional help.

Marty did not get help until he joined a treatment program in prison. He had been sentenced to seven years in prison and 15 years of probation for the sexual abuse of his daughter.

Professional Services.

If Marty's parents had engaged with professional services, they and Marty probably would have participated in a range of services. These services include family therapy, couples therapy, individual therapy for the parents and Marty, group therapy for Marty, and psychoeducation about sexuality and child development for Marty and his parents. Parents must be willing to do whatever it takes for their children. These are typical services for families when the children have sexual behavior issues.

Many parents are unwilling to do this. Children like Marty are on their own, to their detriment and the detriment of other people.

Extensive Mutual Sexual Behaviors

In Gil and Johnson's typology, extensive mutual sexual behaviors refer to children and young people who engage in sexual behaviors whenever they have the opportunity to do so. They require continual adult supervision. Typically, these children do not force younger children to have sex with them, although some do. They usually either find other same-age children who are as sexualized as they are or they persuade other children to have sex with them. They usually perform sexual behaviors associated with adult behaviors, such as intercourse, oral sex, and anal sex.

These children and young people have many risks and few protective factors. They often have extensive histories of abuse and neglect, many foster home placements, separations from family members, parental abadonments, difficulties in school, poor peer relationships, and an overall sense of failures in many different areas. No one has been there for them consistently, over time.

A NEATS Assessment

In terms of the NEATS, they may have neurological issues that predispose them to problems with executive function and self-regulation. They typically, but not always, have long histories of insecure attachments characterized by abusive and neglectful parents, and with histories of complex trauma. They often have had multiple foster care placements and multiple mental health diagnoses. Their styles of attachment are primarily disorganized as is the attachment style of their parents. In some families, the attachment style may be combinations of ambivalent, dismissive, avoidant, and disorganized.

Disorganization characterizes the course of their lives. Child protective services may have had long-term involvement, but these professional services have not helped these children and young people.

Sometimes children with such histories live in adoptive homes. Adoptive parents require a great deal of information and support. There may be a mismatch between adoptive parents' styles of attachments and the disorganized attachments of their adoptive children. In many cases, family relationships in these situations are difficult. Adoptive parents may find that they are often frustrated, angry, and disorganized themselves.

There is no easy answer to parenting children with these multiple issues. It is clear, however, when these adoptions become satisfactory, the adoptive parents have used many services and are able to detach from their children's difficult behaviors while remaining emotionally responsive and maintaining their roles as executives of their families. These families find that a team approach to parenting works. That means that other people help them in their parenting.

Single parents have a network of supportive persons who provide them with support, understanding, and suggestions for what to do. Members of this network also take over parenting for brief periods to give parents respite. Couples parenting children ideally have a network of supportive persons. In addition, they themselves work as a team, serving as a backup when one of them feels overwhelmed by the stresses of care.

Children who live in treatment foster care require similar kinds of parenting if they are to cope with their complex traumas and to gain their capacities for secure attachments, executive function, and self-regulation. In treatment foster care, the parents are highly trained, highly paid professionals who have the skills to provide children who have disorganized attachment styles with the safety, security, predictability, and structure that children require in order to learn how to function well; in order words, to deal with their complex trauma, to develop capacities for executive function and self-regulation, and to develop secure styles of attachment.

In other words, young people with extensive mutual sexual behaviors young people have not experienced the safety of secure relationships where they develop good executive skills and capacities for self-regulation. No one has helped them to deal with their traumas.

Because they have such trauma-filled histories with little relief, they rarely have consistent capacities for empathy. In addition, on the surface, at least, they may not think there is anything wrong with their sexual behaviors. How they behave is natural to them.

Children live what they have experienced. Often, however, down deep, these children feel worthless, unloved, and insignificant, with an overlay of shame and guilt about their perceived failures and their sexual behaviors. While these children challenge adults how want to parent them, many of them work through their many difficulties in the safety of secure relationships where they and their parents are involved in a network of effective professional services.

Professional Services

Children with extensive mutual sexual behaviors are common in residential treatment and in treatment foster care. Typically, their families of origin have been uninvolved for years. Children and young people require the safety of secure relationships in order to develop good executive functions and prosocial self-regulation. In short, children with mutual extensive sexual behaviors require what they don't have. In fact, they require the very relationships whose lack led to their sexual issues in the first place.

In summary, children with these issues can and do learn to regulate their sexual behaviors if they have long-term secure relationships, structure, predictability, and psychoeducation about appropriate and inappropriate sexual behaviors. Sadly the services they require are in short supply. They often are on their own, to their detriment and to the detriment of others. In addition, society loses what these talented young people might have contributed to the common good.

Children Who Molest

Children who molest force and trick others into sexual behaviors. Like children who have extensive mutual sexual behaviors, children who molest are unable to stop their behaviors without supervision, structure, psychoeducation, and the safety of secure relationships.

Case Examples

The two case examples show different kinds of parental responses to sibling molestation. The first is of a family where the single parent mother was dismissive of her children's behaviors. The second shows a couple who did not believe their three year-old daughter when she said her brother was touching her pee-pee. Years later, they did believe her. The abuse had been on-going.

Twelve year-old Roberto who promised his eight year-old brother Tonio a candy bar if Tonio would suck his dick. Tonio worshiped Roberto and missed him. Tonio had been away from the family for three months. Tonio did not know why. Roberto was in residential treatment for sexually abusing Tonio and three cousins. Roberto was home for the weekend. Their mother Stella let the two boys sleep in the same bed, which showed poor judgment, a sign of inadequate executive function.

Neither Tonio nor Roberto told anyone about the sexual abuse that occurred that weekend. What happened came out a few weeks later, when a girl at Tonio's school told the teacher that Tonio had asked her to suck his dick. Tonio told a child protection social worker about Roberto's recent abuse.

This case shows a common characteristic of families where children molest. The parents have a dismissive style of attachment. They refuse to believe that the sexual behaviors are abusive. In the case of Tonio's harassment of the girl in school, his mother Stella said, "He was just fooling around." She said the Roberto's abuse of Tonio was "just sex play."

Stella herself was an incest survivor and had lived in foster care for a year after she told a teacher about her father's abuse. When her father went to prison for his abuse of Stella, Stella returned home. Her mother accused Stella of breaking up the family.

Stella participated in a sex abuse treatment group as a teenager, but she did not like the group. She graduated from high school and was enrolled in business school when she became pregnant at 19. She dropped out of school, went on welfare, and then disability, and had two more children. She lived with a succession of men who were convicted sex offenders. She appeared not to recognize the risk these men posed to her children.

Another example is the case of seven year-old Rakim, three year-old Lavinia, their mother Julie and father Joe. Lavinia told Julie that Rakin touched her pee-pee. The parents talked things over and asked Rakim if he had touched Lavinia. Rakim said no. The parents believed him. They could not imagine that a seven year-old would do this.

Three years later, two neighborhood teenage girls knocked on the door. Julie answered. The girls told Julie they had been at the playground with Lavinia, now six. They said that Lavinia told them that Rakim touches her private parts and won't stop when she tells him to. Lavinia also said she had told her mother, and her mother did not do anything.

This time, Julie and Joe believed Lavinia. They called their attorney who advised them first to find a relative who would provide a home for Rakim and then to call child protection. She (the attorney) said child protection will refer the family for services and not remove the children if Rakim were out of the home and the family accepted all services. Julie and Joe did what the attorney advised.

The family participated in sex abuse treatment for 16 months. Rakim had group and individual therapy. The parents had family therapy with Rakim, and then family therapy with Lavinia. The children did not participate in family therapy together for several months. The family also received psychoeducation about sexual abuse and sexuality.

When the therapists thought everyone was ready, they arranged a series of reconciliation sessions. Rakim apologized to Lavinia. Lavinia had had excellent preparation for these session.

She told Rakim how angry she was at him and how hurt. Over the course of several sessions, the children and their parents worked on the effects of the sexual abuse. The parents took responsibility for not believing Lavinia years earlier. They told Lavinia how sorry they were.

The parents also had couples and individual therapy. Julie once again dealt with her own history of incest. She thought she had done so when she was a teenager and had participated in family incest treatment. As she thought about it, she realized that her earlier treatment had helped her get through her teen years, to attend college, and to marry Joe whom she loved.

Julie did a lot more work on the effects of the incest. Joe realized that he had not been as emotionally available to his wife and children as he should have been. He worked hard on his own issues with emotional expressiveness and availability.

After a year of treatment, Rakim returned to the home. After four more months of treatment, the family gradually stopped treatment. They now occasionally return to see one of the therapists on an as-needed basis.

Risks and Protective Factors

In this case, the family was fairly well put-together. Rakim had a diagnosis of ADHD, but many children do and few of them sexually abuse other children. Rakim had no known history of sexual abuse. The only explanation that the professionals had about the sexual abuse is the possibility that somehow Julie's family history of incest was transmitted to Rakim. Julie had thought that the cycle of abuse had stopped with her generation. Now she hoped the abuse had stopped with her children's generation.

Joe's emotional distance from the family may have been a factor in Rakim's abusive behaviors. It is remarkable from an outside point of view that she and her husband did not recognize the possibility that Rakim was being sexually abusive to Lavinia. Professionals have seen this kind of blindness many times. They simply accept is as common and are aware the even otherwise well put-together families may not realize sexual abuse is occurring in their families.

Joe and Julie had a committed relationship, and they were committed to their children as well. When they finally realized that Rakim was sexually abusive to Lavinia, they sought the advice of an attorney and did exactly what the attorney advised. This was difficult for them, wrenching, in fact. They felt guilty, remorseful, and fearful of the future. They did everything social service professionals wanted them to do. They fully engaged in treatment and encouraged their children to do.

A NEATS Assessment

In terms of the NEATS, only Rakim appears to have neurological issues since ADHD appears to have neurological origins. He also had issues with attachment, executive function, and self-regulation. His abuse of Lavinia involved these three aspects of the NEATS. He may have experienced stress in his life, but apparently his parents did not offer the safety of secure relationships where he could develop alternatives to sexual abuse of his sister. Had his parents helped him develop executive skills and prosocial ways of dealing with his emotions, he may not have sexually abused Lavinia. Rakim had no known history of trauma.

Lavinia, at three, showed good executive function and secure attachment when she told her mother about Rakim's sexual abuse. When Julie and Joe did not believe her, she may have experienced trauma and a break in her trust of parents. She showed good executive skills when she persisted and told older girls in the neighborhood about her brother's sexual abuse. She required extensive professional help with her trauma and to repair her relationship with her parents and her brother.

Joe and Julie appear to have had a mostly secure relationship between themselves, a relationship that therapy strengthened.

The parents probably thought they had secure relationships with their children, but they did not. They did not provide the safety of secure relationships, and their home was not a safe haven for either child until the family had therapy.

Both parents showed poor executive functions in terms of understanding the abuse the older boy perpetrated on his younger sister. They showed excellent executive skills when they realized that Rakim indeed was sexually abusing Lavinia.

Julie had a history of trauma stemming from incest and the subsequent breakup of her family. She thought she had dealt with the effects of the incest, but the incest in her own nuclear family showed her she had not. As an adult and as a wife and mother, she dealt once again with her own experiences of incest and its effects.

So far, this family has had the best possible outcomes, with the family back together and the parents emotionally available to their children, offering them the safety of secure relationships. They now set clear boundaries for themselves and their children. They enforce the boundaries. They recognize and reward respectful behaviors and teach by example as well as by words how the children are to behave in appropriate ways.

Discussion

Sexual behaviors in childhood span a wide range, from healthy, to inappropriate, to abusive. Sexual development is as natural as other developmental pathways, such as emotional, physical, and neurological. As in any other area of development, children require sensitive responsiveness and guidance if they are to develop healthy sexuality.

Guidance includes both word and deed. Parents must first conduct themselves in sexually appropriate ways. They also talk to their children about sexuality and its appropriate and inappropriate expressions. They encourage children to talk to them.

Parents and other adults understand that children are learners. Children may behave inappropriately as part of developmental processes. Securely attached parents set limits on children's behaviors and guide them to behaving in appropriate ways. Just as children learn to keep their hands to themselves when they are near flames, they also learn to keep their hands to themselves regarding sexual behaviors.

Providing children with what it takes to nurture their sexual development helps build parent-child relationships. As a 14 year-old boy said to his mother, "If I can talk to you about sex, I can talk to you about anything."

The key to healthy sexual development is parental emotional availability and sensitivity. Parents who have these qualities foster optimal child development because they provide children with information and guidance and model appropriate behaviors themselves. Children internalize their experiences with their parents. Children's sexual behaviors mirror their experiences within their families.

Children can learn to cope with adapt to, and over come adversities when their parents are there for them and are willing to do whatever it takes for the sake of their children. Many parents refuse professional help, to the detriment of their children and the persons their children may hurt. Furthermore, society is deprived of the contributions the children may have made as the mature. Spending years preoccupied with sexual issues diminishes opportunities to contribute to the common welfare.

A NEATS assessment and an assessment for risk and protective factors in combination with Gil and Johnson's typology of childhood sexual behaviors are helpful in understanding the various sexual behaviors that children may have. These assessments are also provide guidelines about when to do to raise sexually healthy children.

References

Friedrich, William N. (2007). *Children with sexual behavior problems: Family-based attachment-focused therapy.* New York: Norton.

Gil, Eliana & Toni Cavanagh Johnson (1993). *Sexualized children: Assessment and treatment of sexualized children and children who molest.* Rockville, MD: Launch Press.

Gilgun, Jane F. (2010). Do abused children become abusers? In Jane F. Gilgun, *Shame, blame, and child sexual abuse: From harsh reality to hope* (pp. 132-140). Available at http://www.scribd.com/doc/16484981/Child-Sexual-Abuse-From-Harsh-Realities-to-Hope

Gilgun, Jane F. (2010). Talking to children who have been sexually abuse. Available at http://www.scribd.com/doc/24561563/Talking-to-Children-Who-Have-Been-Sexually-Abused

Gilgun, Jane F. (2010). *The NEATS: A child and family assessment.* Available at http://www.scribd.com/doc/16496944/The-NEATS-A-Child-Family-Assessment

Gilgun, Jane F. (2006). Children and adolescents with problematic sexual behaviors: Lessons from research on risk and resilience. In Robert Longo (Ed), *Work with children and adolescents with sexual behavior issues* (pp. 383-394). Holyoke, MA: Neari Press. Available at http://www.scribd.com/doc/21896410/Children-With-Problematic-Sexual-Behaviors-Lessons-From-Research-on-Resilience

Gilgun, Jane F., Kay Rice, & Danette Jones (2005). Emotion-focused therapy and children with problematic sexual behaviors. In Martin C. Calder (Ed.), *Children and young people who sexually abuse: New theory, research, and practice developments* (pp. 231-244). Dorset, England: Russell House. Availabl at http://www.scribd.com/doc/56713865/Emotion-Focused-Therapy-and-Children-with-Problematic-Sexual-Behaviors

Hindman, Jan (1998). *A very touching book...for little people and big people* (rev. ed.) Baker City, OR: Alexandria Associates.

Hoyle, Sally G. (2000). *The sexualized child in foster care: A guide for foster parents and other professionals.* Washington, D.C.: Child Welfare League of America.

Johnson, Toni Cavanagh (2009). *Helping children with sexual behavior problems: A guidebook for parents and substitute caregivers* (4th ed.). www.TCavJohn.com

Johnson, Toni Cavanagh (2009). *Understanding children's sexual behaviors: What's natural and healthy.* www.TCavJohn.com

Lieberman, Alicia F. (2004). Traumatic stress and quality of attachment: Reality and internalization in disorders of infant mental health. *Infant Mental Health Journal, 25(4),* 336-351.

Lieberman, Alicia F. (2007). Ghosts and angels: Intergenerational patterns in the transmission and treatment of the traumatic sequelae of domestic violence. *Infant Mental Health Journal, 28(4),* 422-439.

Schechter, Daniel set al (2006). Traumatized mothers can change their minds about their toddlers: Understanding how a novel use of videofeedback supports positive change of maternal attributions. *Infant Mental Health Journal, 27(5),* 429–447

Van der Kolk, Bessel A. (2005). Developmental Trauma Disorder: A new, rational diagnosis for children with complex trauma histories. *Psychiatric Annals 35(5),* 390-398.

Van der Kolk, Bessel A. (2005). Developmental Trauma Disorder: A new, rational diagnosis for children with complex trauma histories. *Psychiatric Annals 35(5), 390-398.*

Weatherston, Deborah J., Melissa Kaplan-Estrin, & Sheryl Goldberg (2007). Strengthening and recognizing knowledge, skills, and reflective practice: The Michigan Association for Infant Mental Health competency guidelines and endorsement process. *Infant Mental Health Journal, 30(6),* 648-663.

Wozniak J., Biederman J., & Richards J.A. (2001). Diagnostic and therapeutic dilemmas in the management of pediatric-onset bipolar disorder. *Journal of Clinical Psychiatry, 62,*10–15.

14

Case Planning in Services for Children and Their Families

When children have emotional, psychological, and behavioral issues, service providers recommend a series of actions to guide children toward optimal development. The following is a list of typical recommendations that become part of case plans. The list is based upon the experiences of parents and children, service providers, and research on children and families.

Basic Human Needs

Basic human needs are safety, food, clothing, shelter, and medical care. Service providers may find that they spend considerable time advocating for families to meet their basic human needs. Instability in these areas distracts parents and children from attending to services meant to foster children's optimal development. Conversely, stability in these areas helps the children and their parents to become psychologically available to each other and to services.

Safe, Predictable Families

Children require consistency, love, predictability, structure, and clear guidelines about what adults expect of them. With structure, love, and predictability, children can thrive, especially if they are working with adults who are helping them to manage their behaviors and to deal directly with their traumas.

For children to do well, case planning ensures that such family conditions are in place for children. When parents are able to follow through on the referrals and recommendations that professionals make, parents are able to provide the safety, predictability, and love that children require. Sometimes parents cannot ensure safety and, in fact, behave in such ways that they traumatize their own children.

Family violence and psychological abuse of children are far too common. Parents as perpetrators of trauma is hideous for children. The very persons who are supposed to protect them are the occasions for trauma. Children are trapped. If parents cannot ensure children's safety and are the causes of the lack of safety, foster care and even termination of parents rights are worth considering.

The parenting style that sums up safety, love, and predictability is authoritative parents. When parents are authoritative, they show high warmth to the children as well as high expectations, and they give immediate, brief recognition when children do something they want children to repeat. Penalties for antisocial and inappropriate behaviors are brief, followed by clear explanations of what the children did wrong and how they can do better in the future.

Safe Neighborhoods & Schools

Housing in safe communities with good schools are other considerations related to safety. Finding safe housing in safe neighborhoods can be an important goal in case planning. Schools sometimes are not safe for children when school personnel do not understanding children's issues. The case plan may include goals for educating teachers, administrators, social workers, janitors, and other school staff about children's issues and effective responses. Some school personnel view children's dysregulation as willful defiance and not the results of child trauma or neurological conditions. Rather than providing high warmth, structure, and predictability, their responses may increase children's trauma.

Social Histories

Social histories can help to identify family strengths as well as unattended traumas in children and parents and patterns of family interactions and conditions within nuclear and extended families that contribute to children's issue. Service providers revised case plans as they learn more about family histories. Case plans typically are in operation early in cases before providers and clients have opportunities to explore relevant aspects of family history.

Emerging research shows that some challenging behaviors in childhood are in response to traumas that children may have experienced as infants and toddlers, and parents either did not know how to respond, did not know that they were supposed to respond, or they received erroneous information from professionals about how to respond.

Lieberman (2007) provided an example of Sophia who was 30 months old when she saw a man break into the family home and beat and attempt to rape her mother. Before the attack, Sophia had been verbal, bright, and outgoing, on-track developmentally. After the attack, she became silent, sad, and fearful. Her mother received psychiatric for a year immediately after the attack.

The psychiatrist recommended that the mother not talk to Sophia about the attack and said that Sophia would forget about it. When Sophia's behavior became increasingly of concern, her mother sought an infant mental health treatment program where, after months of enacting the violent scenario over and over, Sophia said to her mother and therapist, "He came in because I did not close the door." Sophia then was 42 months old.

Sophia's self-blame was developmentally appropriate because children her age want to understand why events happen. Their levels of cognitive development lead them to believe that their behaviors are the cause. In other words, they did something wrong, and that's why bad things happen.

Sophia's mother was an attentive parent who sought appropriate help for her daughter. The link between Sophia's behavioral issues and her earlier trauma is clear. Imagine how many children experience trauma early in childhood and no one recognizes it. When the children later show serious emotional and behavioral issues, no one may know why and attribute the issues to other causes. When this happens, interventions may not be helpful and could make problems worse.

Along with the identification of the possible factors contributing to children's issues, social service professionals also look for indicators that the parents and children have capacities for dealing with these issues. For example, parents who have voluntarily sought care for their children and who have advocated for services show capacities for doing what it takes to ensure their children's optimal development. This is the case for Sophia.

Social histories include behaviors, occupations, and life styles over time, not only of parents and parents' siblings, but also of the grandparent generation. By obtaining such information, professionals can get an idea of whether issues are neurologically-based, trauma-based, have some other basis, or are combinations of factors that repeat themselves over generations. For example, in many families, mental disorders such as autism spectrum disorders or attention-deficit hyperactivity disorders are issues for several family members. Such familial patterns suggest neurological predispositions.

If alcohol or drug abuse is present in parents, it is possible that their children have neurological effects such as fetal alcohol spectrum disorders or other outcomes related to fetal brain injuries from the chemicals. As infants and young children, they may also develop behaviors in response to parents' alcoholism that are functional in the family context but cause them problems in other settings.

In addition, children of alcoholics and abusers of other chemicals may have genetic predispositions for chemical abuse. When children and young people have experienced many adversities, have beliefs that justify inattention to others, and few protective factors to off-set their risks, children have alcoholics have a heightened likelihood of having trouble with alcohol and other chemicals later in life, even starting in childhood.

Genograms offer efficient ways of showing intergenerational issues such as predispositions for mental illnesses, anxiety, alcoholism, and other conditions, as these often are transmitted from parents to children. They also provide a picture of intergenerational capacities for effective parenting and life skills.

Social histories also include information about life events that may affect children and their families. Experiences of war, terrorism, and discrimination and oppression can have big effects on parents and children. Such histories also help to identify the actions that parents have taken to protect their children from the negative effects of these events. For example, a disproportionate number of children born to Somali refugees in the United States show signs of autism spectrum disorders. The Somali community, social service professionals, and medical personnel want to know why and are advocating for social policies, programs, and research that will make things better.

Ecomaps can show the various influences on child and family development and functioning and how parents respond. They include factors such as parents' work experiences, relationships with extended families, quality of social services, effects of social policy, membership in religious, volunteer, and self-help organizations, recreation, school and education issues, and neighborhood issues.

Neurological Exams

Neurological issues often underlie children's challenging behaviors. A pediatric neurologist can identify possible neurological conditions and make recommendations for further actions. Neurological exams include evaluations of children's developmental levels and physical coordination as well as brain scans.

A typical recommendation is early childhood family education programs that can begin in infancy and may last for two or more years. These programs involve direct intervention with children, parent education about the children's conditions, and parent involvement in remedial interventions.

Neurologists often prescribe medications as well. Research has shown that combinations of medication, direct intervention with children, and parent education can be of great help.

Medical Exams

Sometimes medical conditions, such as hearing loss and impaired vision, affect children's development. Medical exams can rule out or rule in contributing medical conditions. Simple procedures such as tonsillectomies may be warranted, as well as more complicated surgeries to remedy physical conditions, all of which contribute to child and family well-being.

Parents often require medical attention. Medical conditions, such as diabetes, high blood pressure, and heart trouble may be debilitating to parents and contribute to the psychological unavailability. When they are hospitalized, children may experience the trauma of separation.

Psychological and Educational Evaluations

Psychological and educational evaluations can help to identify other conditions that contribute to children's difficulties. Professionals can make recommendations for further actions, such as types of educational settings that are best suited to the children and whether children require special services, such as personal care attendants. Psychologists can make referrals to various types of therapy and parent educational opportunities.

If children have not had a neurological or medical exam, these professionals can make referrals for these services.

Deal Directly with Children's Trauma

Research shows that trauma does not go away on its own, but must be deal with directly. Children require the safety of secure relationships to deal with the effects of trauma. Treatment plans must present clear strategies for ensuring that children receive the care they need to learn to cope with the effects of trauma.

Unattended child trauma is a threat to optimal child development. Not only do the children suffer when they have experienced trauma, but their efforts to regulate the effects of trauma may result in behaviors that are difficult for parents and other family members. Thus, trauma becomes part of developmental pathways that not only involve the effects of traumas themselves but also the disruptions in attachments, including relationships with parents, siblings, and peers, that result can from dysregulations associated with unattended trauma.

Not all children act out traumas and attempt to self-regulate in antisocial ways. Some self-regulate through internalized responses such as anxiety and withdrawal, while others may behave inappropriately. Children may show all three ways of re-regulation.

The hoped-for developmental pathway for children who have experienced traumas—as well as neurological issues that interfere with attachment relationships such as autism spectrum disorder—in one based on the safety of secure relationships with parents and therapists where children can process their trauma and internalize capacities for coping with dysregulation in prosocial ways. Parent involvement in children's treatment for trauma is key to optimal outcomes for children.

Structured Children's Intervention Programs

Some children benefit from group treatment and psychoeducation that include family involvement. Early childhood family education programs are examples. Parents and children participate in separate educational programs during the first part of the session and then practice the learnings together in the second part of the session.

Programs for children with sexual behavior issues are time-limited groups, lasting about 12 weeks, where four to fix children meet with two facilitators to learn about issues that contribute to their sexual behaviors and practice skills intended to help them manage their sexual behaviors. These programs have components for parents, where parents have psychoeducation about their children's issues and how to respond to them.

Children demonstrate to the parents at the end of each group session what they have learned in that day's group. These programs also offer individual therapy to children and to their parents, couples therapy, and family therapy. Informal multiple family therapy may take place in the waiting area when parents stay while their children are in group.

Day treatment is another kind of structured program for children that requires parental involvement. Much of the program time is devoted to children, but parents are involved to the extent that they carry program learnings into the family settings. Coordination between program and family is the foundation of such programs.

Involvement of Children in Activities They Enjoy

Children want to be involved in activities they enjoy. Professionals can help parents make choices about appropriate activities. Some children require supervision at all times. While this may limit some of their activities, there are others that are open to them. Youth recreation programs, after-school activities, sports, music lessons, and outings to movies, parks, and other recreational facilities on a regular basis can promote child development. Any activity in which children experience success can boost self-concept and self-efficacy.

Parental Participation in Helping Systems

Family and professional experience and research show that children have the best chance of reaching optimal development when parents have the commitment and resources to change their own behaviors in response to the issues their children present. In many families where children have troubling behaviors, parents have unresolved issues that interfere with their competence as parents. In other situations, parents do not have an unusual set of personal issues that interfere with their parenting, but the care of their children overwhelms their personal resources, and they require additional resources and support.

Families who have refugee status or who are members of non-majority ethnic groups often are responsive to services that culturally specific groups and agencies provide. Families who have experienced trauma and social dislocation find that their children have difficulties adjusting to the instability they have experienced.

Parents, too, can be preoccupied with all they have been through and are thus psychologically unavailable to their children. Culturally specific groups and agencies can become safe havens where parents and children find relationships and resources that help them to deal with troubling issues.

Typical parental actions that contribute to children's development include

> o **Psychoeducation.** In psychoeducation groups, parents not only learn about specific children's issues such as anxiety or conduct, but they also have opportunities to share their experiences and to process some of their emotions. These groups also may educate parents on how to manage children's behaviors, including opportunities to practice these new skills. These groups may be time-limited or on going.
>
> For parents of young children, an infant mental health intervention can be an approach of choice. In infant mental health, both the children and the parents participate in the intervention where professionals guide parents to deal with their personal issues that affect their parenting while also teaching parents about child development and how to optimize children development. The interventions take place while parents are interacting with their children.
>
> There also are many effective education and intervention programs available to parents. Professionals may have to do some research to locate them. The Internet is a rich source of information, and parent support groups are helpful to many parents;
>
> o **Parents participate in support groups** where they can process emotions related to parenting, where they can share any helpful actions they have taken, and where they can learn from the experience of other parents;
>
> o **Parents deal with partner issues**. Often, conflicts with marital partners arise in response to children's difficult issues or contribute to children's difficulties. Parents in these situations typically require couples counseling;
>
> o **Parents deal with their own unattended traumas**. In some situations where children have difficulties, their parents have histories of unresolved traumas. These issues interfere with parents' capacities for sensitive responsiveness to their children. They may have dismissive, preoccupied, or disorganized styles of adult attachment that engender insecure attachments in their

children, such as avoidant, ambivalent, and disorganized child attachment styles.

Secure attachments between parents and children are the foundation for optimal development. Therefore, it is of high importance to encourage parents to deal with their own issues, if not for themselves, for the sake of their children. If parents are not able to do this, their children may do all right in life because they find other people who substitute for emotionally available parents, but they would do much better if their parents had attended to their own resolved issues.

o **Parental chemical dependency treatment.** This can be a challenging referral to make because sometimes parents require in-patient treatment. Who will care for the children? Who will pay for treatment? How tolerant are social policies for parental relapse? How do the children cope with separations from parents?

o **Family therapy.** This approach is meant to repair damaged relationships, to guide parents to have effective responses to their children's behaviors, and for parents and children to practice new behaviors in the session; and

o **Parents deal with their physical health** when it interferes with their functioning and parenting. Many parents of children with challenging issues have medical issues that they may neglect because of the demands of parenting. Service providers can be of great help in supporting parents to get the medical care they require.

John's parents are examples of a couple whose tensions affected their capacities for attunement to their traumatized child. His parents were estranged from each other. His father spent his free time on the Internet where he was having a emotional "affair." His father also was depressed and used alcohol frequently. His mother felt depressed and anxious about her partner's behavior, but she did not talk to him after her froze her out when she did try. Instead, she frequently was preoccupied with her partners' behaviors talked to her mother and sister about her concerns. She often was psychologically unavailable to John.

At six, John began to act out sexually. His parents immediately sought professional help. John had been sexually abused two years earlier by the husband of a day care provider. John had also seen the man molest other children. A social history showed a fairly well put-together family that was middle-class, educated, and law abiding.

Scattered throughout the family tree were individuals who had issues related to anxiety, depression, and chemical abuse, but most family members showed good mental and physical health. The family had resided in the same home for ten years, had stable work histories, and well-paying jobs.

The professionals John's parents consulted made the kinds of recommendations discussed in this book, and his parents followed through. They arranged for a neuropsychological exam for John, which was largely negative except for anxiety and issues with self-regulation related to the sexual abuse and sexual acting out. The psychologist noted that parents in the neighborhood would not allow their children to play with John because of his sexual behaviors.

This increased John's anxiety and made him sad. The psychologist thought that, given John's competence in many areas such as wanting friends and being personable and outgoing, this situation might help motivate him to participate fully in treatment.

John's parents enrolled him in a sex-specific treatment program that included individual therapy for John, family therapy, couples therapy, and a 12-week psychotherapy group for John. Parents participated in the last 15 minutes of the one-hour group so that the children could show the parents what they had learned during the session. John's father quit drinking, saw a psychiatrist, and began taking anti-depressants. His mother did individual therapy where she learned how to manage her own anxiety.

The parents reported that they were falling in love again. Both parents became psychologically available to John who told his father that he thought his father did not love him because the father did not pay attention to him. The father was heartbroken and said, "John, I love you with all my heart. I'm so sorry you thought I didn't."

John showed remarkable gains in managing his sexual behaviors and his anxiety. Parents of children in the neighborhood once again allowed their children to play with John. The changes in John's behaviors paralleled the changes in his parents' behaviors.

Education & Advocacy About Social Policy

Sometimes parents are unaware of social policies that can benefit them and their families, such as special education programs, income support, and housing. Social service providers are positioned to educate parents about these supports and to advocate on behalf of families. There are local chapters of national organizations for such issues as children with developmental disabilities and children with mental illnesses.

Involvement in Informal Networks

Parents' and children's involvement in social, religious, cultural, self-help, and volunteer networks can be an important part of case planning. These networks contribute to quality of life by providing a sense of belonging, an identity with larger issues, and a place where other people know you. Self-help groups such as Al-Anon, Al-A-Teen, and Narcotics Anonymous are tailored to issues that are common to children and families where chemical abuse is at issue.

Refugee families benefit from networks of refugees who have arrived earlier and who can facilitate adjustments of the newly arrived families. Some religious organizations, based in churches, temples, and mosques, groups have made life-changing contributions to the lives of struggling families, providing emotional support and respite and sometimes even food, clothing, and shelter.

Parents of children with serious issues may become preoccupied with parenting to the point where they rarely spend time away from the family. This can lead to social isolation, which can affect energy levels, motivation, and mood. Involvement in informal networks can be beneficial to parents who feel alone, afraid, and hopeless.

Parental Self-Care

Parenting is difficult even with the most optimally functioning children. When children present challenges beyond what is typical, parents have to be vigilant about self-care. Just as the airlines directs passengers to put oxygen masks on before they help others, so parents have to take good care of themselves so that they can be sensitively responsive to their children. Therefore, a case plan would encourage parents to participate in recreational activities, to socialize with other adults, to have hobbies they enjoy, to take time for themselves, to use respite care when available, and to eat balanced meals, sleep well, and exercise.

Discussion

Parenting children with emotional, psychological, and behavioral issues is demanding. Service providers can be of help when they make recommendations and referrals to services that can support children and families. This brief chapter outlines some of the services and actions that research, family experience, and professional experience have shown to be effective. Parental sensitive responsiveness is key to optimal child development. Parent supports have immediate beneficial effects on children.

Sometimes parents are overwhelmed with services; that is, service providers from different agencies may make home visits several times a week. In these situations, collaboration and service coordination among providers make sense. Collaborations that work and parents who respond to case plans are hopeful signs that the parents and children are going to reach an even keel. Services are haphazard and service provider conflicts harm families. Service providers are temporary; parents are forever. The goals of services are to help parents become psychologically available to their children and to become independent of social services. That is one of many reasons that informal support systems are important.

Parents often work, and this places limitations on the time they have to respond to case plans. Because of work demands, they may require more time to complete the plan, although in some child protection situations, time could be an issue.

Further Readings Related
to the NEATS

A science-based framework for early childhood policy: Using evidence to improve outcomes in learning, behavior, and health for vulnerable children. (2007). Cambridge, MA: Center for the Developing Child at Harvard University. http://www.developingchild.harvard.edu/content/downloads/Policy_Framework.pdf. Retrieved on September 23, 2008.

Anderson, Peter (2002). Assessment and development of executive function (EF) during childhood. *Child Neuropsychology, 8(2),* 71-82.

Cicchetti, Dante & Blender, Jennifer (2006). A multiple levels-of-analysis perspective on resilience: Implications for the developing brain, neural plasticity, and preventive interventions. *Annals of the New York Academy of Sciences, 1094,* 248-258.

Cicchetti, Dante & John W. Curtis (2007). Multilevel perspectives on pathways to resilient functioning. *Development and Psychopathology, 19,* 627-629.

Davies, Douglas (2004). *Child Development: A practitioner's guide (2nd ed.).* New York: Guilford.

Dawson, Geraldine (2008). Early behavioral intervention, brain plasticity, and the prevention of autism spectrum disorder. *Development and Psychopathology, 20,* 775-803.

Georgieff, Michael K. (2007). Nutrition and the developing brain: Nutrient priorities and measurement. *American Journal of Clinical Nutrition, 85 (2),* 614s-620.

Hinshaw-Fusilier, Sarah, Neil W. Boris, & Charles H. Neanah (1999). Reactive attachment disorder in maltreated twins. *Infant Mental Health Journal, 20(1),* 42-59.

Hohman, Melinda, Rhonda Oliver, and Wendy Wright (2004). Methamphetamine abuse and manufacture: The child welfare response. *Social Work, 49(3),* 373-381.

Koren-Karie, Nina, David Oppenheim, & Rachel Getzler-Yosef (2004). Mothers who were severely abused during childhood and their children talk about emotions: Co-construction of narratives in light of maternal trauma. *Infant Mental Health Journal, 25(4),* 300-317.

LeDoux, J. (2002) *Synaptic self: How our brains become who we are*, New York, Penguin.

LeDoux, J. (1996). *The emotional brain*. New York, Simon and Schuster.

Lieberman, Alicia F. (2004). Traumatic stress and quality of attachment: Reality and internalization in disorders of infant mental health. *Infant Mental Health Journal, 25(4)*, 336-351.

Mash, Eric J., & David A. Wolfe (2006). *Abnormal child psychology* (3rd ed.). Belmont, CA: Wadsworth (Thomson Learning)

Massaro, An, Rebecca Rothbaum, & Hany Aly (2006). Fetal brain development: The role of maternal nutrition, exposures and behaviors. *Journal of Pediatric Neurology, 4(1)*, 1-6.

Shields, A. and Cicchetti, Dante (1998) Reactive aggression among maltreated children: The contributions of attention and emotion dysregulation, *Journal of Clinical Child Psychology, 27*, 381-395.

Shirilla, Joan J., & Deborah J. Weatherston (Eds.) (2002). *Case studies in children's mental health*. Washington, D.C.: Zero to Three.

Sokol, Robert J., Virginia Delaney-Black, & Beth Nordstrom (2003). Fetal Alcohol Spectrum Disorder. *JAMA, 290(22)*, 2996-2999.

Teicher, M. H. (2002) Scars that won't heal: The neurobiology of child abuse: Maltreatment at an early age can have enduring negative effects on a child's brain, *Scientific American, 286*, 68-76.

Internet Resources

Amen Clinics: http://www.amenclinic.com

Autism Speaks. www.autismspeaks.org An especially informative website

Autism Society of Canada: http://www.autismsocietycanada.ca/asd_research/asc_initiatives/index_e.html

Center for Early Education and Development, University of Minnesota, Twin Cites, USA. http://cehd.umn.edu/CEED/

Child Trauma Academy. http://www.childtrauma.org/ctamaterials/Professions.asp

Medline Plus:
http://www.nlm.nih.gov/medlineplus/childmentalhealth.html

National Institute of Mental Health:
http://www.nimh.nih.gov/health/topics/child-and-adolescent-mental-health/index.shtml

Trauma Center at Justice Resource Institute:
http://www.traumacenter.org

About the Author

JANE F. GILGUN, Ph.D., LICSW, is professor, School of Social Work, University of Minnesota, Twin Cities, USA. She has done research on how children, adolescents, and their families cope with adversities for more than 25 years. She has published widely, most recently on the NEATS assessment.

She has presented locally, nationally, and internationally on resilience, violence, and treatment approaches that build on client competencies. She has developed many assessment tools based on her research.

Professor Gilgun has a Ph.D. in child and family studies from Syracuse University, a master's in social work from the University of Chicago, and a licentiate in family studies and sexuality from the Catholic University of Louvain, Belgium. In addition, she has a bachelor's and master's degree in English literature with a major in British and American poetry.